Steps to the Great Perfection

Steps to the Great Perfection

The Mind-Training Tradition of the Dzogchen Masters

Jigme Lingpa

With contributions by
Garab Dorje and Longchenpa

Translated and introduced by Cortland Dahl

Foreword by Tulku Thondup

SNOW LION
BOULDER
2018

Snow Lion
An imprint of Shambhala Publications, Inc.
4720 Walnut Street
Boulder, Colorado 80301
www.shambhala.com

9 8 7 6 5 4 3 2 1

First Paperback Edition
Printed in the United States of America

⊚ This edition is printed on acid-free paper that meets the
American National Standards Institute Z39.48 Standard.
♻ Shambhala Publications makes every effort to print on recycled paper.
For more information please visit www.shambhala.com.

Distributed in the United States by Penguin Random House LLC
and in Canada by Random House of Canada Ltd

Designed by Gopa & Ted2, Inc.

The Library of Congress catalogues the hardcover edition of this book as follows:
Names: 'Jigs-med-gling-pa Rang-byung-rdo-rje, 1729 or 1730–1798, author. |
    Garab Dorje. | Klong-chen-pa Dri-med-'od-zer, 1308–1363. | Dahl, Cortland,
    1973– translator, editor. | Thondup, Tulku, writer of foreword.
Title: Steps to the great perfection: the mind-training tradition of the
    Dzogchen masters / by Jigme Lingpa; with contributions by Garab Dorje
    and Longchenpa; translated and introduced by Cortland Dahl; foreword by
    Tulku Thondup Rinpoche.
Other titles: Thun mong gi sngon 'gro sems sbyong rnam pa bdun gyi
    don khrid thar pa'i them skas.
English
Description: First Edition. | Boulder: Snow Lion, 2016.
Identifiers: LCCN 2015030982 | ISBN 9781559394543 (hardcover: alk. paper) |
    ISBN 9781559394772 (paperback: alk. paper)
Subjects: LCSH: Rdzogs-chen.
Classification: LCC BQ7662.4 .J58513 2016 | DDC 294.3/420423—dc23
    LC record available at http://lccn.loc.gov/2015030982

These key instructions on the preliminary practice
of the seven mind trainings
Serve as steps that lead to the primordial nature.

—Longchen Rabjam,
The Essence of Luminosity

Contents

Foreword

ACCORDING TO BUDDHISM, every being is a composite of mind and body. Our mind is who we are. Our body is a precious but temporary abode where our mind lives and functions as long as we are alive. As soon as we die, our mind, or consciousness, leaves our body and takes rebirth. Whether this rebirth is happy or painful depends solely on whether the effects of our past karmic deeds are positive or negative. The important point is that if we train our mind on the path of profound teachings, such as Dzogchen, our mind will become free from emotional flames and karmic bondage and will awaken to its innate wisdom.

The main text in this precious volume is the teaching on the seven mind trainings entitled *The Steps to Liberation*, composed by Rigdzin Jigme Lingpa. *The Steps to Liberation* explains the seven mind trainings revealed in two Dzogchen tantras entitled *The Sole Offspring* and the Precious Copper Letters, and in their commentaries by Garab Dorje and Longchen Rabjam.

Mind trainings are generally regarded as preliminary trainings (Tib. *ngondro*) that are done before the main body of meditations. However, as this volume teaches, we can also practice any of the seven mind trainings as a main body of meditation by uniting it with esoteric meditation exercises to accomplish higher attainments.

Let me summarize how this is done with the first of the seven mind trainings—impermanence. We first develop a heartfelt experience and understanding that every facet of life and every compounded entity in the world is momentary and changing. We let that heartfelt conviction rouse us to meditate on, and pray to, the lama with earnest devotion and genuine trust. We then visualize that a beam of blessing light comes from the lama's heart. By its mere touch at our heart, our consciousness is freed from our body and united with Guru Padmasambhava in his lotus of light pure land of the three-fold buddha-bodies. With loving-kindness and compassion to all, we develop confidence that we have attained the power to lead all beings to the attainments that we have reached. We then mindfully rest in the state that is fully open.

It is thanks to impermanence that we can improve our lives and attain the highest goals. When we truly realize that everything is impermanent, our mental attachments and aggressions spontaneously fade away. It opens us to esoteric meditations and realizations such as pure perception, devotion, and unity with the true nature. Phadampa said,

> When (the realization of) impermanence is developed
> in your mind-stream, first, it causes you to enter into
> Dharma. In the middle, it whips you to be industrious.
> Finally, it makes you to attain the luminous dharmakaya.[1]

Longchen Rabjam said,

> The merits of realizing impermanence are infinite:
> You will abandon the faults of samsara and accumulate all
>   the virtues naturally.
> You will be freed from grasping at concepts of eternity and
>   will dissolve attachments to loved ones and hatred to
>   foes.
> You will swiftly attain the nectar-like deathless state
>   (buddhahood).[2]

Steps to the Great Perfection is a treasure of profound teachings revealed by the greatest masters of the Dzogchen lineage. Synthesizing both common and esoteric meditations, it offers profound trainings for both beginners and advanced meditators to attain high realizations. Cortland Dahl has offered a great service for English readers of Dharma by presenting another ambrosia-like volume with great clarity and beauty.

TULKU THONDUP

Translator's Introduction

IN 2001, I MOVED from the United States to Nepal to study the Tibetan language and to spend time meditating in retreat. I had been practicing Buddhism for nearly ten years at that point. Over the course of those ten years, I learned of Tibet's four main Buddhist lineages—the Nyingma, Sakya, Kagyü, and Geluk Schools—and of the great masters who had safeguarded these lineages for more than a thousand years. Looking back, I remember how difficult it was to keep all the names of these masters from blurring together. I recall being struck by their teachings on emptiness and pure awareness, and humbled by their teachings on compassion. Perhaps more than any other set of teachings, however, I remember being deeply moved by the mind-training (Tib. *lojong*) teachings that were brought to Tibet in the eleventh century by the great Indian master Atisha (980–1054 CE).

In contrast to the complex philosophies of Mahayana Buddhism and the impenetrable imagery of the Vajrayana, I found the mind-training teachings to be refreshingly straightforward and accessible. In teachings such as Geshe Chekawa's *Seven-Point Mind Training*, Langri Tangpa's *Eight Verses on Training the Mind*, and Atisha's own *Lamp for the Path to Enlightenment*, I discovered countless gems of practical advice.[1] Their instructions teach us how to let go of pointless pursuits and focus ourselves wholeheartedly on practicing the Dharma. They encourage us to open our hearts to the suffering of others and to make the awakening of all beings our primary mission in life. They even call into question our mostly deeply held beliefs about ourselves, about the world, and about the nature of experience. I struggled to put these teachings into practice but found in them an inexhaustible source of guidance and inspiration.

Atisha's teachings became the basis for the Kadampa lineage. Though the Kadampa lineage did not survive as an independent tradition, its precious heritage was incorporated into other lineages. The textual tradition became a cornerstone of the Geluk lineage and inspired one of Tibet's literary masterpieces, Je Tsong Khapa's *The Great Treatise on the Stages of the Path to Enlightenment*.[2] The practice lineage of the Kadampas was similarly incorporated into the Kagyü lineage by the great master Gampopa (1079–1153), who immersed himself in the teachings of the Kadampa masters prior to meeting his root guru Milarepa (1052–1135). Not only have the mind-training teachings been preserved over the centuries, in the present day, they are widely taught throughout the world and by many of Tibet's most esteemed teachers, including His Holiness the Fourteenth Dalai Lama and His Holiness the Seventeenth Karmapa, Ogyen Trinley Dorje.

By the time I arrived in Nepal, I was well aware of the importance of Atisha's teachings and had experienced their transformative power in my own life and practice. I could also see their influence in the practices that I was learning in the Nyingma lineage. My daily practice at the time was focused on the preliminary practices (Tib. *ngondro*) for the Heart Essence of the Vast Expanse, a cycle of teachings that was revealed in the eighteenth century by Jigme Lingpa.[3] Though not formally drawing on the Kadampa teachings, these preliminary practices borrowed heavily from Atisha and his heirs. When I read the classical instructions on the preliminary practices, and when I heard Tibetan lamas explain them, the mind-training teachings were often quoted and inspiring stories of the Kadampa masters were commonplace. It was clear that these teachings had permeated the entirety of Tibetan Buddhism.

What I did not realize at the time was that Atisha's lineage is not the only tradition of mind-training teachings found in Tibet. Not long after I arrived in Nepal, I had the good fortune to meet one of the great living masters of the Nyingma lineage, Chatral Rinpoche, a reclusive yogi who has spent decades meditating in solitary retreat. Chatral Rinpoche gave me permission to practice the preliminaries of the Heart Essence of the Vast Expanse and sent me to Kyapchen

Tulku Rinpoche, one of his main students, to receive further instruction. Unfortunately for me, I could not yet speak or read Tibetan, and Kyapchen Tulku Rinpoche spoke no English. This state of affairs was great motivation, however, so I redoubled my efforts, determined to improve my Tibetan to the point that I could receive teachings on the preliminary practices.

As luck would have it, I got to know another remarkable lama at this time, a great scholar from Tibet named Khenpo Sherab Sangpo. Khenpo was learning English at the time and also happened to be deeply learned in, among other things, the exact same lineage that I was beginning to practice. Every day I would help him with his English, and then we would switch roles and he would teach me how to read Tibetan texts. Together, we read through Jigme Lingpa's commentaries on the preliminaries in their entirety.

Jigme Lingpa wrote three commentaries on the preliminary practices. Two of the texts, *How to Practice* and *The Application of Mindfulness*, are pithy instructions on the outer and inner ngondro practices, respectively.[4] When I first began reading these texts, they felt very familiar, and for good reason: they were the basis for *Words of My Perfect Teacher*, the classic text on the preliminaries that I had read in English numerous times. They were also similar in both style and substance to many of the mind-training teachings from Atisha's lineage.

In addition to *How to Practice* and *The Application of Mindfulness*, Jigme Lingpa wrote a more lengthy work entitled *The Steps to Liberation*. When I started reading this text, I was pleasantly surprised to find that it was a commentary on the seven-point mind training. I assumed that this was the same seven-point mind training from the Kadampa masters and was excited to find a commentary on these practices by one of my spiritual heroes.

It turned out that I was completely wrong. Once I began reading, I found a set of mind-training instructions that were entirely different from those that I studied in other lineages. There was no mention of the traditional mind-training texts that I was already familiar with. Instead, there were references to the Precious Copper Letters, the *Child Scripture*, the *Luminous Tantra of Self-Manifesting Awareness*, and other scriptures that I had never heard of. The contemplations were also very different. There were discussions of important principles like impermanence and karma, yet along with these discussions were contemplations filled with symbolic imagery. These were not the typical visualizations found in other forms of Buddhist tantra either. I had never read anything quite like them, nor have I seen anything like them since.

The most striking difference, however, I found at the end of Jigme Lingpa's work. The seventh mind-training exercise departs from the format of the first six and extends into practices that work with the energies and channels of the subtle body, and even into explorations of the nature of awareness itself. These topics are typically found in advanced meditation manuals for those who have already undergone a lengthy training process, but here they were in a book on the preliminary practices. I was surprised and intrigued. The teachings I had stumbled upon, while similar in name, bore almost no resemblance to the mind-training teachings I was familiar with.

Though I did not know it at the time, this was my first glimpse of a profound mind-training lineage that stretches back to the very earliest Great Perfection instructions, the most treasured teachings of the Nyingma lineage. This glimpse opened my eyes to the wealth of mind-training teachings found in the Nyingma School and especially to those associated with the Heart Essence (Tib. *Nyingtik*) of the Great Perfection. There are many unique and interesting features of the Great Perfection mind-training teachings. In some ways, they are very similar to the Kadampa instructions. They are pithy and direct, and experiential rather than scholarly. They also distill the most essential teachings of the Buddha into a practical system that can easily be implemented in a daily meditation routine, as do Atisha's instructions. At the same time, they bring together the most foundational Buddhist teachings with the incredibly profound methods of the Vajrayana (the esoteric teachings of Buddhist tantra). This is the hallmark of Dzogchen mind training and what sets it apart from other mind-training lineages.

I spent more time reading Jigme Lingpa's commentary on the seven points of mind training with Khenpo Sherab Sangpo. Eventually, I was able to discern the history of the teachings. It turns out that Jigme Lingpa's work is an expansion of a short text by Longchenpa, the greatest Tibetan master of the Great Perfection. Longchenpa's teachings refer to an obscure text by Garab Dorje, the first human teacher of the Great Perfection, and Garab Dorje's teachings, in turn, are a commentary on a single line from *The Tantra of the Sole Offspring*, the root text of an important cycle of teachings that were brought to Tibet in the eighth century by the Indian master Vimalamitra (exact dates unknown).

I found it quite astonishing that a single line from an obscure, esoteric text became a precious seed that would eventually flower as the pith advice of three remarkable awakened beings. Later, I would find that other important masters, including Jamyang Khyentse Wangpo (1820–92) and Jamgön Kongtrul (1813–99), also wrote on these same teachings.[5] Though not often taught, it is clear that these pith instructions inspired some of the most influential masters of the entire Buddhist tradition.

The teachings on the seven mind trainings by Garab Dorje and Longchenpa, as well as *The Tantra of the Sole Offspring*, were included in an important collection of Great Perfection writings by Longchenpa. This collection came to be known as the Fourfold Heart Essence and is considered the most thorough and authoritative set of texts on the practice of the Great Perfection ever compiled.[6] It contains the Great Perfection instructions that were brought to Tibet by Padmasambhava in the eighth century—a cycle known as the Heart Essence of the Dakinis—and also a set of instructions taught around the same time by Vimalamitra—the Heart Essence of Vimalamitra. To the root texts of these two traditions, Longchenpa added a multitude of commentaries that he wrote himself.[7]

The seven mind trainings that I mentioned above form part of the preliminary practices in the Heart Essence of Vimalamitra. These teachings, both the instructions on the preliminary practices and also those on the various main practices of the Great Perfection, are incredibly precious. In Tibet, they have been carefully preserved for centuries. To the few with the good fortune to practice them, these pith instructions have been taught with the utmost care, often in the context of strict retreat, where they can be integrated with experience under ideal circumstances. Encountering these teachings was seen as an occurrence that is exceedingly rare. Even among the most cherished teachings of Tibetan Buddhism, these particular instructions are held in the very highest regard by practitioners of the Great Perfection.

In the pages that follow, you will find translations of the root verse on the seven mind trainings from *The Tantra of the Sole Offspring*, along with commentaries on these practices by Garab Dorje, Longchenpa, and Jigme Lingpa. With these translations, you will see the unique perspective that each of these great masters brings to the same set of teachings. You will also see for yourself how these teachings have grown from a small seedling into a beautiful flower. Though the fragrance of this flower has most certainly been diminished by my inadequate efforts to render these teachings in English, I sincerely hope that you find them as profound and transformative as I have.

ACKNOWLEDGMENTS

This work would not have been possible without the blessings of Chatral Sangye Dorje Rinpoche. Rinpoche introduced me to the world of the Longchen Nyingtik and gave me permission to translate these teachings and to make them available to others. For his boundless blessings and compassion, I will be forever grateful. I am equally indebted to Yongey Mingyur Rinpoche, who has guided my study and practice and given me countless opportunities to deepen my experience of the teachings. I can never hope to repay his kindness. In addition, I would like to thank the following teachers for contributing to this book in various ways: Dzogchen Ponlop Rinpoche, Kyabje Trulshik Rinpoche, Kyapchen Tulku Rinpoche, Matthieu Ricard, Semo Saraswati, Shechen Rabjam Rinpoche, and especially Tulku Thondup Rinpoche for writing the foreword for this book. Last but certainly not least, I would like to offer my heartfelt gratitude to Khenpo Sherab Sangpo, spiritual director of Bodhicitta Sangha. In addition to deepening my understanding of the Dharma through the many teachings I received from him, Khen Rinpoche sat patiently with me and explained Jigme Lingpa's text line by line when I read it for the first time. Later, I was fortunate to translate for him as he gave teachings to a small group of students on this very same text. Throughout, I was able to ask him countless questions to clarify difficult passages and explain obscure points in the text. Without his blessings and guidance, translating these works would not have been possible. If anything of the profundity of the Great Perfection teachings has made its way into this book, it is due solely to the blessings of these gifted teachers.

I would also like to express my gratitude to all those who helped improve the quality of the translation. First and foremost, I would like to thank Heidi Nevin for proofing my translation and providing excellent editorial feedback and Anne Klein for sharing her passion for these teachings and offering helpful suggestions about the translation. I would also like to thank Franka Cordua-von Specht, Greg Johnson, Bonnie Lynch, Mark Moore, and Kate Thomas for proofreading the text and offering helpful feedback, Renee Ford for helping with the glossary, and Michael Wakoff at Shambhala Publications for editing the final manuscript.

This work would never have seen the light of day were it not for the generous support of many individuals. I would especially like to thank all those who supported the Rime Foundation from its inception in 2004 until 2009, when it was absorbed into Tergar International. I would also like to thank the Khyentse Foundation for partially sponsoring this project. Finally, I would like to express my gratitude and thanks to my wife and Dharma partner, Kasumi Kato, and my son C.J. I can't imagine what my life would be like without their love and support.

Whatever goodness comes of this project I dedicate to the flourishing of the Great Perfection in all times and places, to the long lives of the masters who uphold its teachings, and to the enlightenment of all beings. In the words of Longchenpa:

> Through this virtue, may all beings throughout existence
> Awaken together, without a single being left behind.

In the pure realm of the luminous essence, the ground of
    the Great Perfection,
May they remain inseparable from the kayas and wisdoms.

TSULTRIM SHÖNU (CORTLAND DAHL)
Madison, Wisconsin
February 2015

STEPS TO THE GREAT PERFECTION

Excerpt from
The Tantra of the Sole Offspring

———————•——————

Training the mind in these stages
Will join impermanence with the mind.[1]

Excerpt from *The Secret Commentary on the Tantra of the Sole Offspring*

Garab Dorje

THE MEANING OF the line "Training the mind in these stages . . ." is as follows: "The mind" refers to oneself. "Stages" refers to the seven forms of mind training, in which one trains in bodhichitta by contemplating:

1. The impermanence of all conditioned phenomena
2. Fleeting and lasting happiness
3. The various circumstances that can cause death
4. The pointlessness of all mundane endeavors
5. The virtues of the Buddha
6. The guru's instructions
7. Nonconceptuality

"Training" refers to having practiced each of these mind trainings for three or twenty-one days. The meaning of "[This] will join impermanence with the mind" is as follows: "[This]" refers to the seven forms of mind training. "Impermanence" means "to gain certainty." "Join . . . with the mind" means that the first training in bodhichitta will turn your mind away from samsara, the second will make you repulsed by suffering, the third will arouse the prerequisite of faith, the fourth will allow you to engage the guru's instructions, the fifth will give you resolve in meditation, the sixth will keep you from engaging in negative activities, and the seventh will cause your meditative concentration to develop.[1]

The Seven Mind Trainings

ESSENTIAL INSTRUCTIONS ON THE
PRELIMINARY PRACTICES

Longchen Rabjam

To the guru and yidam deity, along with the host of dakinis,
I pay homage with the utmost respect, in body, speech, and
   mind.
As a way to access the nature of the manifest essence,
I will now elucidate the essential instructions of the seven
   mind trainings.

To ENABLE fortunate beginners to gradually access the nature of
manifest awareness, the Precious Copper Letters presents seven
forms of mind training that pertain to the following topics:

1. Impermanence
2. Fleeting and lasting happiness
3. The various circumstances that lead to death
4. The pointlessness of all mundane endeavors
5. The virtues of the Buddha
6. The guru's instructions
7. Nonconceptuality

1. CONTEMPLATING IMPERMANENCE

On an outer level, time is impermanent. The four seasons come
and go. Day and night come and go as well, changing moment by

moment. On an inner level, the four aggregates and the four elements are impermanent as well. Constantly changing, they are as fragile and insubstantial as a mass of bubbles. On a secret level, your parents and loved ones are impermanent and will die.

When will you find yourself in the same situation? There is no way to be sure that you will not die this very day or tomorrow. Without getting distracted for even a moment, ask yourself wholeheartedly, "I wonder if I will die this evening, or perhaps tomorrow?" All sentient beings that you see will die as well, so meditate on the thought, "When will these beings pass away?"

Contemplating in this way will help you to see that all conditioned phenomena are impermanent by nature. Seeing them as examples of impermanence will help your mind become more focused. This is the way to gauge whether or not you have mastered this practice. The purpose of meditating in this manner is to turn your mind away from samsara.

2. CONTEMPLATING FLEETING AND LASTING HAPPINESS

Negative acts produce the lower realms and all forms of suffering, whereas virtue creates the higher realms and all forms of happiness. By their very nature, the higher and lower states of samsara are like the paddles on a waterwheel. Fluctuating and ephemeral, samsara is deeply flawed. The most profound way to avoid being caught up in samsara is to attain enlightenment and liberation. Everything else is unreliable and deceptive.

On the other hand, if you enter the path of liberation, you will attain the temporary pleasures of the higher realms and sublime qualities will take birth in your being as they have in the bodhisattvas. You will attain the lasting happiness of supreme enlightenment just like the buddhas. For these reasons, you should think, "I must achieve temporary and ultimate sublime happiness!"

If you do not enter the path of liberation, nonvirtue will lead you to the lower realms. Even if the virtue you have practiced leads you to a birth in the higher realms, you will eventually have to journey through the lower realms. When you think wholeheartedly that all activities end up causing suffering, you will have familiarized yourself with this mind training. The purpose of meditating in this way is to elicit a feeling of disenchantment and disillusionment with the suffering of samsara.

3. CONTEMPLATING THE VARIOUS CIRCUMSTANCES THAT LEAD TO DEATH

When born in samsara, there is nothing that you can rely on or trust. When you try to help someone, you may be harmed in return. Even food and drink can lead to illness or death. Whatever material wealth you manage to hoard could end up fulfilling the desires of your enemies and thieves. Hoping that your friends and loved ones will help you, you may imagine that they will bring you benefit, but these same people may become your worst enemies. Or, even if they do not actually harm you, they may insult you or disparage you for no reason. Whatever you do, it will not satisfy others. Indeed, worldly activities are endless and deeply problematic.

If you sincerely consider the attitudes and behavior of others, you will see that though you may try to help them, some will be satisfied while others will not. No matter how you look at it, you can see with certainty that all of this is useless. All that you do is imbued with the nature of suffering. There are innumerable circumstances that lead to illness and death. As these circumstances do not produce any real benefit, the only infallible objects to rely on are your guru and the Three Jewels. For this reason, if you cultivate devotion and make offerings to them, you will be setting in motion the causes of happiness.

Think to yourself, "I must focus solely on virtue!" With this in mind, reflect on all the good and bad circumstances of the past, what you are doing in the present, and what you will do in the future. Cultivate a sense of disenchantment, and focus your mind. When compassion toward all six classes of sentient beings manifests and you enthusiastically think of all your activities as an offering to the Three Jewels and your guru, you will have mastered this mind training. Meditating this way serves to elicit the prerequisite of faith.

4. CONTEMPLATING THE POINTLESSNESS OF ALL MUNDANE ENDEAVORS

The day you die, all of the things that you have done in your present life will do you no good. This includes protecting your loved ones, thwarting your enemies, engaging in farm work, seeking to profit from business dealings, pursuing material gain and fame, getting caught up in attachment and aversion, benevolently counseling others, chasing after influence and a good reputation, making friends and enjoying material pleasures with your loved ones, and making a home for yourself. Indeed, everything that you have done in the past is now nothing more than a memory. Like last night's dream, it won't come again. What you experience today is like this evening's dream, while all that you will do tomorrow will be like tomorrow night's dream. What a waste to have spent your time on pointless pursuits: getting caught up in attachment and aversion, quarreling with others, hoping to hear pleasant things and not to hear anything unpleasant, pursuing pleasure and avoiding pain, accumulating and hoarding things, and so on.

5. CONTEMPLATING THE VIRTUES OF THE BUDDHA

For the fifth mind training, think to yourself, "The Buddha transcended all the shortcomings of samsara. His form radiated the marks and signs of complete enlightenment, his speech turned the wheel of Dharma, while his mind never wavered from the state of wisdom. Indeed, he was the sublime guide of the entire world, including the gods; he was its sole protector and support. For these reasons, I must attain buddhahood as well, for without doing so, I will not be of any benefit. Moreover, since buddhahood cannot be attained without meditating, it is essential that I do so. I must practice with perfect concentration, following the example of the amazing, accomplished masters of the past, who endured hardships and lived in isolated places on their quest for liberation. Just as they did, I must cast aside all the activities of this life and practice alone in a remote place!"

You will have mastered this practice when you think, "I must meditate, since without doing so it won't be possible to attain buddhahood." This will serve to strengthen your resolve in meditation.

6. Contemplating the Guru's Instructions

For this mind training, ponder the reasons for practicing the guru's instructions. Consider how the guru is the one who will guide you across the boundless ocean of samsara to liberation. The guru's instructions, like a great vessel, will liberate you. For this reason, you should practice your guru's teachings to the letter, for if you do not, you will be perpetually tormented by the illness of suffering. With great affection, the guru is like the king of doctors. You must practice the guru's nectar-like instructions diligently day and night.

You will have mastered this practice when you think, "What's the point of all the things I do in this present life? I should practice the guru's instructions and nothing else!" This will keep you perfectly focused on your guru's instructions, without getting caught up in other activities.

7. Contemplating Nonconceptuality

The Nonconceptuality of Bliss-Emptiness

To train the mind in the nonconceptuality of bliss-emptiness, imagine the syllable HAM at the upper end of your central channel and an AH syllable at your navel. Fire blazes forth from the AH and hits the HAM, causing a stream of nectar to descend, filling the four root chakras and all the secondary chakras. This, in turn, causes bliss-emptiness to arise. As you visualize this, pull the lower energy up, press the upper energy down, and focus on a white AH syllable at your heart center. This will produce the empty knowledge that utilizes the skillful means of bliss.

The Nonconceptuality of Clarity-Emptiness

To train the mind in the nonconceptuality of clarity-emptiness, begin by expelling the stale breath three times. As you inhale, imagine that all external appearances and objects melt into light, merge with blue space, and then completely fill your entire body. Finally, join and hold the energies. This will generate clarity-emptiness. A vital point of this practice is to meditate that the energies are hot if a cold sensation is dominant, and cool if a hot sensation is more intense. Because different energies are active in different seasons (summer is associated with the fire energies, fall with the wind energies, winter with the water energies, and spring with the earth energies), there are more elaborate meditations that work with the energies that remedy these sensations, as well as on different forms and feelings. The energy of space, however, is good to practice at all times, and as physical sensations are included in these two (hot and cold), this is sufficient for practice.

The Nonconceptuality of Reality Itself

To train the mind in the nonconceptuality of reality itself, relax the body and mind from deep within. Without moving your eyes, meditate in a state free from the comings and goings of thoughts. By meditating in this way, you will be able to concentrate on whatever you direct your attention to, after which you will be able to rest for longer and longer periods in a nonconceptual, space-like state. When this comes to pass, you will have mastered this practice. This helps to develop bodhichitta more and more.

May the virtue, as pristine as a snow mountain,
From this work on the seven forms of mind training,
These vital points on the exceedingly profound preliminaries,
Lead all beings to the state of total peace.

Through the propensities of having trained in lives past,
In this life I have mastered the essential meaning of the
    Supreme Vehicle.

Therefore, with the wish to benefit others in mind,
I have revealed and clarified the profound nature.

Fortunate ones, regard this point of entry
To the profound, essential meaning as your crown ornament.
The sublime path, the chariot of those who desire liberation,
Will be swiftly accomplished based on these words.

These essential instructions on the preliminary practice of the seven forms of mind training were composed on the slopes of the Kangri Tökar by Longchen Rabjam, a yogi of the Supreme Vehicle.

These teachings have been entrusted to the glorious protectress of mantra Ekajati, Za Rahula, and the Oath-Bound Vajrasadhu. Should these teachings be corrupted with other words or changed, may they mete out a harsh punishment! Keep this secret from those who are not fit vessels! Grant it to those who are worthy!

Secret!
Samaya!
Virtue, virtue, virtue!

The Steps to Liberation

ESSENTIAL INSTRUCTIONS ON THE COMMON PRELIMINARY PRACTICE OF THE SEVENFOLD MIND TRAINING

Jigme Lingpa

Homage to glorious Samantabhadra!

Your nature is perfectly and utterly pure, unconfined and
  unrestricted;
Unborn, unobstructed, and free of all elaboration, the innate,
  primordial mind of enlightenment.
It is timeless, an unconditioned and unchanging dimension
  with all supreme qualities.
Beyond samsara, nirvana, and identity, Primordial Protector,
  with your six special characteristics, to you I bow.[1]

The display of your manifest ground is like the moon's
  reflection in water.
Your magnificence brings the ocean of existence to maturity.
Manifest in the dimension of luminosity, a net of magical
  illusion,
Second buddha Padmasambhava, I make this offering to you.

Leader of humankind, lion among men, king of the Shakyas
  and your heirs;
The six ornaments—the two chariots and so forth—and two
  supreme ones, the sole eye of the world Shantarakshita,

The seven tested men, glorious Dipamkara, Shakyashri, the
    Omniscient Fifth, and so on—
Foundation of the teachings, masters of the three levels of
    discipline, how could I not have faith in you?

Teacher of the Supreme Vehicle, Lord Garab, empowered and
    anointed with total dominion by the heroic Lord of Secrets;
The five eminent holy beings, King Ja, empowered with the
    eighteen volumes of tantra;
Vimalamitra, master of the true lineage of the three yogas,
    Vairochana, and the rest of the twenty-five disciples
Who opened the door to the vast and profound from the
    treasury of the fivefold expanse, transcending one hundred
    limitations—in you I have heartfelt faith.

The subjects expressed—the twelve divisions of the Buddha's
    teaching,
And their meaning—emptiness, devoid of inherent existence,
Comprise the Buddha's teachings of transmission and
    realization.
In this snowy land, the one who clarified and mastered these
    teachings was the omniscient Lord of Speech, to be sure.

When the entire range of instructions, the doctrines of sutra
    and tantra,
Are understood in a single sitting, this is the consummation
    of the teachings.
Uniting with the wisdom mind of the dharmakaya, free of
    any effort or strain,
Is the unique richness of Dzogchen, the Great Perfection.

Therefore, among the infinite instructions of this tradition,
The common preliminary practice of the seven mind trainings
I shall carefully explain using the three valid cognitions,
Without falling into the extremes of being too brief or too
    long-winded.

THE NATURAL Great Perfection is the victorious summit of all vehicles. With its six unique lineages, the infinite number of approaches that comprise the traditions of sutra and tantra can be explained in a single sitting. The common preliminary practice of the seven mind trainings provides access to this Great Perfection.

Concerning these essential instructions, my own guru, the omniscient Santapuripa, true representative of the great master Padmasambhava, stated:

> The meaning of all the Victorious One's sublime words that
>   lead to the higher realms
> Constitutes the path of the lesser practitioner,
> While the meaning that is expressed in all the various
>   teachings
> That show how to work toward the attainment of
>   liberation
> Comprises the path of the middling practitioner.

In light of the classifications outlined here, this particular teaching is grouped under the path of the middling practitioners and below. Nevertheless, the essence of the path that is taught in the main practice is that of the Supreme Vehicle. Considering the inconceivably powerful momentum that is created each time one arouses the motivation of the Great Vehicle, the unique feature here is that bodhichitta is cultivated from the very outset of the path. For this reason, there is no contradiction in classifying these teachings as belonging to the path of the superior practitioner.

This categorization of the three types of practitioners was taught by the uniquely divine Dipamkara in his *Lamp for the Path to Enlightenment*. It was Atisha, a master of awareness with power over longevity, who took on the lifestyle of a celibate in order to propagate the teachings on abandonment and realization as found in the Three Collections.

In truth, there is no real difference between these approaches, for in essence they are merely different ways of employing certain Buddhist terms. It was this understanding that led to [Atisha's approach] becoming less prevalent in the Ancient Translation School. These traditions have been established by those whose penetrating intellects stand up under scrutiny and by the great teachers of the past. Hence, this approach makes it possible to freely explain the teachings by understanding that all the teachings of sutra and mantra should be practiced to the letter.[2]

The sutras state:

> Manjushri, the karmic obscurations of abandoning the sacred Dharma are subtle. Manjushri, to think that some teachings of the Thus-Gone are good and that some are bad is to abandon the Dharma.

As this quote points out, at times people become biased toward certain teachings. They form misguided ideas about teachings that are actually completely perfect and employ a whole series of contradictions and lies to prove their inauthenticity. This sets the stage for them overbearingly to belittle teachings on ethics, thinking that the Vehicle of the Great Secret does not have a structured path to follow. Hearing it taught that all phenomena lack inherent existence, they revile and show hostility toward the authentic path and form the idea that it is not even Dharma. Hence, this presentation also protects such individuals from the abyss of such extremely negative behavior.

In certain scriptures, such as the *Kshitigarbha* and *Perfection of Knowledge* sutras, it is taught extensively that the first gateway to interdependent origination is to respect and venerate the teacher and the teachings. As the *Samantabhadra Tantra* teaches:

> As a disciple, when you first request vows and teachings
> From your guru, you should do the following:
> Wake early in the morning, wash your hands and mouth,
> And don your garments with scrupulous care.
> Prepare by carefully distinguishing those Dharma siblings
> Who possess intact samaya vows and those who do not,
> Then sprinkle water and sweep the teaching courtyard.

As stated here, you should carry out the three types of cleaning:
Begin by bathing and putting on fresh clothes. Those Dharma sib-
lings who do not hold intact samaya vows should then be dismissed
and skillfully avoided. Finally, in accordance with the season and
custom of the land, you should clean the area where the teachings
are being held. Next:

> Arrange a lofty throne with a tasseled parasol above,
> And a vast array of outer and inner offerings.
> In arranging the offerings, it is particularly excellent
> To speak enthusiastically and have a relaxed mind.
> Then, exhort the guru to turn the wheel of Dharma,
> By facing him or her and sounding the conch nine times.
> All the students should supplicate with love.
> Welcome the guru with incense and instruments,
> And request him or her to sit on a comfortable seat.

In this way, without slipping into an attitude of contempt, set out
offerings that will please the guru and the Three Jewels, arrange a
high throne, and so forth. Then, face your guru and sound the conch
to exhort him or her to teach the Dharma, doing so as though you
are making an offering. It is said that many sentient beings who hear
this sound will be liberated from the lower realms. Thus, perform
these acts with the knowledge that the sphere of activity and skillful
methods of the buddhas and bodhisattvas are inconceivable. This is
why sounding the conch to signal the beginning of all sessions is such
an important point.

At that time, the guru should act in a manner that will inspire his
or her disciples. As stated in the *Tantra of the Clear Expanse*:

> Whether the disciple's devotion is great or small
> [Depends on whether] the guru's actions are good or bad.
> Train in the skillful methods for daily activities,
> Such as walking, moving, resting, and eating.

Furthermore, in the context of explaining the samaya vows from the ocean of collected tantras, it is said:

> If the master degenerates, there is no way to train another,
> And both will go to the Hell of Incessant Torment.

Thus, one should train in acting appropriately at all times. This is especially true when one is teaching the Dharma or engaged in a similar activity; one must avoid acting in a careless or inappropriate manner. The *Tantra of the Clear Expanse* states:

> Thus, when teaching the profound Dharma
> To a disciple who is an appropriate vessel,
> The guru should behave as follows:
> Sit cross-legged on a comfortable seat,
> Visualize yourself as the primary mandala
> Of the vehicle that you are teaching,
> And imagine that all the six classes of beings,
> Without exception, appear in an instant before you.
> In accordance with their native languages and mind-sets,
> Teach the Dharma of the Great Vehicle and arouse
>   bodhichitta.
> Politely request all benevolent Dharma protectors
> To help promote goodness and keep obstacles at bay,
> Commission each with enlightened activities.
> Leave the middle of the Dharma assembly empty,
> And imagine that all the forces of good, humans and non-
>   humans alike,
> Listen devotedly to the sacred Dharma.
> With your eyes, gaze upon all the students
> And place your hands [in the mudras] of teaching the
>   Dharma and meditative equanimity.
> Uttering pleasant words, lucid and clear,
> Explain by interweaving examples, their meanings, and
>   rationale.
> In a step-by-step manner, teach the vehicle and approach
> That best match the capacities [of the students].

The tradition of teaching the Dharma as outlined here provides a framework for the vehicle that is taught. To start, you should abandon all careless bodily actions, such as leaning to the side, lying down, and so forth. To prepare for the teachings, place your hands in the mudras of meditative equanimity and teaching the Dharma (the left and right, respectively). When you are teaching the preliminaries, visualize yourself as Shakyamuni, and when you are teaching the main practice, visualize yourself as the lord of the mandala that is specified in whatever tantra, scripture, or key instruction you are teaching. Then lay a foundation for the teaching with the momentum generated by the intention to bring all sentient beings to a state of complete purity.

At this point, imagine that all the six classes of sentient beings have come to listen to the Dharma and are seated before you. In particular, leave an empty space in the middle of the teaching courtyard, and imagine that all benevolent nonhuman beings are gathered and are respectfully listening to the Dharma. Then commission the enlightened activities of pacifying obstacles and promoting goodness.

You should also recite demon-annihilating mantras to deal with the desire-realm gods and their cohorts. According to the *Sutra Requested by Sagaramati*, such mantras render these forces incapable of creating problems for up to a hundred *yojana*s.[3] Abandon "thorns" to the ear, such as speaking too slowly, too quickly, or unclearly. Speaking clearly, lucidly, and pleasantly, explain the connection between the examples, their meanings, and their underlying rationale.

Explaining statements of definitive meaning from the outset and engaging in the activities of union or liberation while still harboring doubts oneself will make the mind of the disciple intractable. For this reason, such things should be avoided. As stated in the *Tantra of the Clear Expanse*:

> When a guru cares for a student,
> The novice student, endowed with faith,
> Must be guided skillfully at the beginning.
> Until the essence of the definitive meaning has been grasped,
> Teachings on both cause and effect should be taught.

> With stories, metaphors, treatises, songs, and the like,
> Cultivate weariness with samsara and explain
> The suffering of the lower realms, the excellent qualities
> Of the Buddha, and other such topics.
> The guru should conduct himself or herself with care,
> For if he or she is caught engaging in union or liberation
>   while uncertain,
> The small-minded will lose faith and be left behind,
> And the student will receive no other blessings.

Therefore, be aware that this contemplative practice is an extraordinarily skillful method for training the mind of the novice practitioner.
    At the time of the main practice, the same text reads:

> Unravel and explain the vajra verses.
> Group and explain the disarrayed tantras.
> Straighten and explain the coils in the transmissions.
> Differentiate and explain the words and significance
> Of the true and concealed intents, the intent for future
>   entry,
> The provisional and definitive meanings,
> And the meanings of the essential and nondual,
> Of the tantras, scriptures, and key instructions.
> Without pointing your finger in the dark,
> The teachings should penetrate the student's mind.
> Just like enabling a blind man to see,
> Practical experience will lead to conviction.

As stated here, vajra verses should be explained with the intent of the true lineage, and the disarrayed tantras should be grouped together like pearls on a string. Straighten the kinks in the transmissions like a snake relaxing its coils. Reveal the hidden key instructions like the sun clearing away darkness, and use logical analysis to differentiate the transmissions and significance of the provisional, definitive, and concealed intentions. The four rivers of special transmission that flow through the Ancient Translation School and the undiminished continuity of teachings on the Sutra, Illusion, and Mind should be explained as taught in the Omniscient Lord of Speech's ocean of instructional treatises.

The stages of the path should be taught in terms of the preparation, main practice, and conclusion. For each stage of the path that is taught, at each chapter or teaching-session break, the essential meanings of all the words should be summarized and condensed into points that can be cultivated in meditation. Be sure to mingle the teachings with the mind of the student.

Whenever appropriate, recount the life stories of the siddhas of the past and tell wonderful tales that are both necessary and relevant. This will eliminate any boredom and drowsiness, reveal students' hidden flaws, and so forth. Imparting key instructions that skillfully tame students enables all of the guru's compassion and blessings to blend with the student's mind like a clay figure being taken from its mold.[4]

In particular, begin each session by cultivating bodhichitta and conclude by sealing the session with a reference-free dedication and aspiration prayers. These are the unique features of the Buddhist tradition. As stated in the *Tantra of the Clear Expanse*:

> At the time of a session break or a break in the text,
> Condense the teachings from start to finish and distill their
>   essential meaning
> Into stable points that can be cultivated in meditation
> And understood as an object of contemplation.
> At certain times, clear away boredom
> With traditional stories and other interesting discourse.
> In order to draw out the student's hidden flaws,
> Insert the small key of traditional tales.
> Afterward, dedicate and make aspirations.
> Treasure all with love and bodhichitta.
> If one is skilled in teaching the practices in this manner,
> The guru will be like a mold of the Buddha,
> The Dharma, like its engravings,
> And a worthy student, like the clay placed inside,

Which will then be marked with the mold's engravings,
Instantaneously transforming into a three-kaya clay figure!
These practical instructions for the master should be held
    in the highest esteem.

Having completed all of the important and minor preparations and practices outlined above, without staining the Dharma with one's own presumptuous fabrications, the students should offer a mandala. Next, lay the groundwork for what follows by thinking with unswerving dedication: "In order to bring all the infinite number of sentient beings to the state of unsurpassed, perfect, and genuine buddhahood, I will enter into this path and strive toward the fruition of the natural Great Perfection, the victorious summit of vehicles and quintessence of all the eighty-four thousand collections of Dharma, the nectar-like teachings of our Blissful Teacher!"

Furthermore, the sutras teach: "Listen extremely well and keep the teachings in mind." Accordingly, abandon the three faults of the vessel, and cultivate the six metaphorical notions that you are a patient, that the Dharma is medicine, that the teacher is a doctor, that diligent practice is the medical treatment, that the Thus-Gone is an enlightened being, and that the Buddhist tradition is a long, healthy life. The *Samantabhadra Tantra* states:

Position yourself cross-legged on a comfortable seat,
And from this pure spot, do not move.
If you have a hat on, place it before you,
And if your hair is up, let it down.
Join the palms, place them in the posture of equanimity,
And abandon all activity with your hands.
With your eyes, gaze upon the teacher's face.
With your ears, listen to the teacher's words.
With your mind, resolve the words and their significance.
When in doubt, ask for clarification.
With your voice, avoid all whispered chatter.
Avoid stretching your legs, reclining, acting pompous,
Sitting on unassigned thrones and raised seats.

Do not cover your head if not ill,
Carry weapons when there are no enemies,
Carry a staff though not elderly,
Or do anything else that is improper.
Place and connect each word with its meaning.
As the focal point at the end of the teaching session,
With great resolve, link the beginning and the end.
Abandon all mundane activities, and be attentive
To the precepts of the Dharma, as taught in the scriptures.

As stated here, bring the correct motivation and conduct clearly to mind and then listen to the teachings. If you use other sets of key instructions, such as those found in the Fourfold Heart Essence, as the source for your teachings, first inspire the students according to their abilities by explaining the superiority of the teachings and the lineage succession.

Impermanence

The *Child Scripture* states:

> Reflect on the fact that all conditioned phenomena are
> impermanent.

SCRIPTURE-BASED CONTEMPLATION

The fact that you have this precious human existence with its freedoms and endowments is due solely to all the positive things that
you have done in the past. If you consider the various metaphors for
this attainment, its relative improbability, and its essence, you will
see how rare such a fortunate state of existence is. What if one of
the unending circumstances that you encounter kills you this very
evening, and tomorrow morning there is nothing but a corpse left
in your bed?

For the most part, the ignorant never give a second thought to
their mortality. They meet death having lived their entire life in a
state of obstinate narcissism. On the other hand, there are some who
are aware that they will die someday yet wish to enjoy themselves
until they grow old. Employing various rituals and methods, they
devote themselves entirely to their plans, hopes, and fears, and are
completely caught up in the aims of their present life. We also busy
ourselves with preparations for the months ahead, gathering provi-
sions, and making other short-term arrangements, but is there any
assurance that we won't have taken on a completely different form

of existence when the future comes? Do we know for sure that we will not end up with horns on our heads and tusks in our mouths, without even the bones of our present bodies left? Indeed, there is no such assurance.

When the moment of death is upon us, there is nothing that we will be able to do. As stated in the *Sutra of Advice to the King*:

> Great king, if the four solid, stable, lofty mountains in the four directions were to crumble to the ground, pulverizing all the grass, trees, and living beings and heaping them up, it would be no easy task to flee quickly, to hold them back by force, to deceive them with wealth, or to reverse their course with certain substances, mantras, and medicines. The same goes for the sickness, aging, death, and decay experienced by all sentient beings. When these four great fears are upon us, it is no easy task to flee quickly, to hold them back by force, to deceive them with wealth, or to reverse their course with certain substances, mantras, and medicines.

Hence, we are all sure to die. The *Sorrow-Dispelling Sutra* says:

> The bodies of the buddhas are adorned
> With the marks and signs of enlightenment.
> If even their vajra bodies are impermanent,
> Then why even mention those with bodies
> That resemble the stalks of plantain trees?

Even our own teacher Shakyamuni, who mastered birth and death, in the end lay down on his deathbed to tame those who cling to permanence. How sad! The same goes for the scholars, siddhas, kings, and ministers of India and Tibet, all of whom were emanations of bodhisattvas. Now all we can do is recount tales of their exploits on behalf of the teachings and teach the superficial stories found in history books, biographies, and annals of the tradition. At the same time, we can see that there is not a single one of these beings alive today. How depressing! And so it is with our acquaintances who were alive a year ago, or in months gone by, and who have since passed away and moved on to their next lives. When they pass away, our friends, family, and those we did not know leave only their names behind. Not even their corpses remain. We can see from all this that we are sure to die as well.

We now find ourselves in a dark age. Even if we manage to live out our allotted life span, our lives get shorter by the day. After twenty-one thousand breaths, our lives are one day shorter; after thirty days, a month shorter; and after twelve months, a year shorter—our lives run out with no difficulty.

The *Sutra of the Vast Display* states:

> The three realms are impermanent like an autumn cloud,
> And the birth and death of beings like watching a dance.
> The lives of beings flash by like lightning in the sky.
> Swiftly and quickly they go, like water cascading down
>   a cliff.

Carefully consider that nothing has the power to stay still for even a moment. Cultivate intense diligence as if your hair were on fire. Be sure to take advantage of this opportunity!

KEY INSTRUCTIONS

In this section, the mind is trained with practical key instructions. Individuals who already have some comprehension of the Dharma will be able to invoke a sense of weariness by examining scripture. This is the best approach for such individuals, as it will impact their minds. The mind of the novice practitioner, on the other hand, will be more intractable, so it must be enticed with examples, stories, and more accessible methods. This is a profound point—[the manner of teaching] must match the character of the student!

To begin, imagine that you have arrived in a fearful, unrecognizable land—an extremely vast plain devoid of human activity, with only the sound of the blowing wind and rustling grass around you. You are completely forlorn and do not know what to do.

Out of nowhere, two beings appear: a white man and a black

woman. "In the City of the Illusory Six Senses," they tell you, "there is a precious, wish-fulfilling gemstone of various colors. To get it, one must cross a great sea by boat. Shall we three journey together to get it?" they ask.

This arouses your interest and you follow them. Traveling on and on, you eventually find yourself in the middle of a great ocean, blue as far as the eye can see. Its size is incalculable and its waves surge up into the sky. The waters of this ocean are filled with sights that your eyes have never beheld—sea monsters, whales, mermen, water horses, and all sorts of terrifying creatures with mismatched bodies and heads.

Tossed about by the waves, you grow extremely frightened and try to escape, yet your burning desire to get the jewel drives you to set off in a ship helmed by these two individuals. You now find yourself having barely reached the center of this great ocean, nowhere near its far shores, when a fierce and overwhelming storm develops. Stricken with fear, the two exhausted rowers paddle madly, until suddenly their oars collide and break apart.

At times, the waves surge into the sky and it feels like the ship is soaring to the very peak of existence. At other times, you find yourself floating in the trough as the waves tower above, as if you have sunk to the depths of the ocean. At this point, there is nowhere to run and escape, no one to call for help, and nothing to hold on to for security. The fear of death hits you, and you realize that it could strike suddenly at any moment, even as you draw your next breath.

Since you have never given any thought to your own mortality, you lack the confidence that comes from practicing the Dharma. From this day on, you will be separated from your children, wealth, relatives, countrymen, and neighbors. They won't do you a bit of good! "How frightening! How terrible! Alas, oh no, oh no!" you cry out in distress.

In the midst of all your cries and lamentations, your kind guru appears in the sky before you in the form of the Great Master of Oddiyana, Pema Tötreng Tsal.[1] Swaying in a gentle dance, he exclaims, "You have believed that samsara is like a wish-fulfilling jewel, but it is painful by its very nature. This is what happens when you never think about your mortality. Your present perception that clings to things as real and solid stems from the ignorant belief in the notion of an individual self. The deceptively seductive man and woman you met are your innate and imputed ignorance. This great ocean is the boundless ocean of samsara. The ship is the aggregate of your defiled illusory body, which is as fragile as a water bubble. The two oars smashing into one another and breaking apart is this human life that ebbs away with each passing day and night and cannot be prolonged once exhausted.

"O fortunate child, it won't suffice just to die. If dying were just like throwing a stone down a well, as the Jains and Nihilists believe, then all would be well and fine. But even the smallest of the positive and negative acts that you've accumulated will affect you without fail, like a plumb line dropped straight down. What are you going to do?"

Hearing this, your fear and suffering intensify, and you pray with one-pointed concentration to your guru. When you have no idea what to do, a whitish light, like a diffuse web, emerges straight from the guru's heart and pierces your own. The ship flips over and your mind leaves your body. Then, in the Three Kaya Palace of Lotus Light, you merge inseparably with the Great Master of Oddiyana and attain buddhahood. Through this, you have the good fortune of being able to lead all the sentient beings that are tormented by the fear of causes such as these.

Once you have imagined all this, relax and leave your thoughts of the three times to themselves, without support. Then, whether your mind is active or at rest, simply maintain a state of mindful awareness.

Karma

From the *Child Scripture*:

> Ponder the fact that all activities manifest as the causes of
> suffering.

SCRIPTURE-BASED CONTEMPLATION

The *Sutra of One Hundred Actions* states:

> The joys and sorrows of living beings
> Are karma, the Sage has taught.
> Karma comes in various forms,
> And, from it, the variety of beings.
> They take on and wander in various forms;
> Thus is the great web of karma.

There is no question that all the joys and sorrows, the good and bad,
the wholesomeness and negativity that we experience are due solely
to our own karma. All the activities of this life create dissonance.
Defeating enemies, protecting loved ones, seeking profit through
farming or business, pursuing wealth and influence, acting out our
lust and anger, offering loving advice to others, working for a living
and making a name for ourselves, and so on; none of this is anything we can rely upon or trust. Though we may do various things
and manage to become prosperous, our own prosperity may end up

fulfilling the desires of our enemies and thieves. While we may eat and drink, hoping to sate our desires, what we ingest may reactivate an old illness and become the cause of our own death. Hoping they will bring us some benefit, we may hold certain people dear and strike up friendships, only for them to become our worst enemies. Although we have not harmed them or done anything else to them, they may bad-mouth us, ridicule us, belittle us, criticize us, and put us down—all without reason. On the surface of things, it seems like everything has the nature of suffering, for all these activities end up causing us nothing but grief. What a great loss that we have not grasped this fact until now!

Now, if we think carefully, we will see that everything we have ever done is gone and will not come back; it is nothing more than a memory, an image in our mind like last night's dream. Even what manifests today is like tonight's dreams, and all that we will do tomorrow is like tomorrow night's dream. Nothing lasts. Yet we still become obsessed with these pointless appearances, whiling away our time as we act out our passion and aggression; quarrel, flatter, and insult; hoard and accumulate material things; experience pleasure and pain; and indulge our prejudices. We end up with nothing but a mass of shortcomings! By their very nature, all worldly appearances are seductive illusions. What a loss that we believed them to be permanent, stable, and unchanging. "I won't concern myself with what happens from here on out," we should think sincerely to ourselves. "Instead, I will look at the problems that clinging to a self creates!"

Key Instructions

Imagine that you have arrived in a distant and foreign land, with no idea how you got there, and no idea where to go. As you sit dazed and confused, eight young men appear on the scene, all of them strangers.

"We have come from an isle shrouded in darkness, that of the all-ground," they say. "In a place that takes many months and years to reach, there is a jewel island. There is a gem that surpasses the imagination there. To get it, you must journey with no regard for the difficulties involved. Isn't this what you seek?"

Their words spark your interest and soon you have joined them on their trip. At times you are caught up in fierce storms, while at other times you must make your way along steep defiles, beset by dangerous beasts and lost in raging torrents. With an empty stomach and thoroughly fatigued, you continue on day and night, assuming your life will be a long one. Finally, when your days are coming to an end and your hair and beard have turned white, you make it to the Island of Jewels and find a variety of amazing treasures. Completely overjoyed, you turn back and head home.

Three days away from home, you come across seven savage bandit brothers on the Plain of the Four Gatherings. They snatch away the jewels that you searched for with such hardship. They strip the clothes from your body and bind your limbs tightly with chains, stabbing you viciously with arrows, spears, swords, and other sharp weapons.

"You with bad karma!" they yell, "If you have a guru, supplicate! If you have a yidam deity, arouse its compassion! If you have a dakini or Dharma protector, call out for help! If you don't have any of these, meditate on the fact of death! You have now reached the border between this life and the next!"

Hearing this, you grow despondent. "Alas! I've thought of nothing but this life and encountered such hardship, yet it has all been pointless. What injustice! I have reached the end of this precious life. Meeting murderers in this desolate land, I have no one to go to for refuge or protection, no friend and no hope for survival. All the hardships that I put myself through have not done me the slightest bit of good. I won't live out my days, for death has suddenly arrived. Alas, how frightening and pathetic it all is!"

As you cry and wail mournfully, the Great Master of Oddiyana appears in the sky before you in a form endowed with the four mudras. Light radiates from his body, driving the savage men far away, and then it is reabsorbed.

"You unfortunate being!" he says. "This is what happens when you are obsessed with samsaric activities as though they are delicious divine nectar when, in fact, they are like deadly poison. The eight men whom you did not recognize are the mounts of the eight collections of consciousness that seduce you away from the wisdom of your own awareness. The jewel you found on the treasure island is the ephemeral happiness of this life. This happiness is like a dream. It does not last. All the hardships that you endured are the sufferings that you so eagerly accept and that lay a foundation for this deception. The changing of the color of your hair and beard signifies the exhaustion of your life, which you wasted in a state of delusion, perceiving suffering as pleasure. The bandits' attack on your life on the Plain of the Four Gatherings signifies your affliction by the 424 illnesses and your life force being taken away against your will by Yama, the Lord of Death. Oh, with bad karma like yours, whatever you do in pursuit of mundane obsessions will end up like this when you meet your demise!"

Hearing these words, intense regret wells up for all that you have done in the past. Understanding that all the pursuits of this life entail nothing but suffering by their very nature, you pray ardently to the Great Master of Oddiyana. As you take all this in, light rays emanate from the master's heart and penetrate your own like iron hooks. At that moment, you are instantly reborn in the land of the Palace of Lotus Light as an enlightened guide capable of leading all sentient beings. Once you have completed this visualization, simply rest your mind in its natural state.

Suffering and Compassion

The *Child Scripture* states:

> Cultivate compassion for the six classes of sentient beings, make offerings to the Three Jewels, and engage in virtuous, wholesome deeds.

At this point, you may have some understanding of death and impermanence and that all activities entail suffering by their very nature. Nevertheless, if you have not yet grasped the key points of spiritual life, your appetite for food, clothing, wealth, and worldly riches will be insatiable, and you will rationalize your need for all these things by saying that they are necessary for practice. Once you get one thing, you'll need something else, and you will do whatever it takes to get the various things that feed your bad habits. There are many who spend their entire lives preoccupied solely with the eight worldly concerns.[1] For this very reason, you must contemplate the sufferings of samsara and cultivate compassion for the six classes of beings.

The *Application of Mindfulness Sutra* states:

> In samsara, you will never find
> Even a needle tip's worth of happiness.

Samsara is suffering, pure and simple. It is devoid of happiness. This is especially true when it comes to the unbearable suffering found in the lower realms, about which Shantideva wrote:

> When taking into account the sufferings
> Of hell and the other lower realms,
> The weapons, poisons, fires, ravines,
> And foes faced by those in the desire realm
> Simply cannot compare.

If our karma simply disappeared without a trace when we died, like a candle going out or a mound of dry grass burning up, then all would be well and good. But like it or not, we will be reborn. In fact, up until now, we haven't done many of the things that render the mind lucid and at ease, and these are the very things that cause rebirth in a fortunate state of existence, nor have we done many of these things in our previous lives. What we are experiencing now is a direct result of that. What's more, we have already accumulated an inconceivable amount of negativity just by playing around! If this results in experiencing the sufferings of the lower realms, then there isn't the slightest difference between what is occurring in this life and what will occur in our next existence.

THE SUFFERING OF THE HELLS

Letter to a Friend reads:

> If we suffer just from seeing pictures of hell,
> And from hearing, remembering, and reading about it,
>   or putting it into form,
> Then what need is there to mention what will happen
> When we experience this intolerable ripening for
>   ourselves?

If you neglect to contemplate these sufferings by applying them directly to your own experience and simply observe the suffering of others as though you were watching a show, true compassion will not arise in your mind-stream. For beginners, it is even difficult for compassion to arise toward sentient beings of their own kind, so you should meditate by cultivating an internal experience, as though you yourself are experiencing the suffering. This approach is also mentioned in the *Last Testament* of the Great Perfection, which states:

Bring to mind the suffering of the six realms.

The Eight Hot Hells

To contemplate this topic, imagine that you have arrived in a strange and desolate land, on the face of a massive snow-covered mountain with a solid sheet of ice below you. Plunged into pitch darkness, you begin to feel extremely cold. As soon as you get the urge for warmth, you are reborn in the hot hells, instantly transported, as in a confused dream. The ground below you is red-hot iron, and you are completely surrounded by terrifying, burning metal. There is no way to tell down from up, as the whole place is filled with red, flickering flames.

In this raging expanse, first you find the Reviving Hell, where there are an incalculable number of sentient beings, all of whom resemble you. Overcome with anger, you beat each other with weapons, and your bodies end up being chopped into hundreds and thousands of pieces. The unbearable pain is so intense that you occasionally fall unconscious. Just when you think you are about to die, a voice from the sky bellows, "Revive!" and you return to your previous condition. You undergo these extremely intolerable forms of suffereing over and over again.

In the Black Line Hell, the fearsome guardians of hell mark eight lines on your body and cut along them with sharp saws. The pain is unbearable, and you scream in agony and long to escape.

Next, meditate on the Crushing Hell. You find yourself between mountains shaped like the heads of bulls, lions, goats, and sheep. You are squeezed between them like egg shells being crushed and streams of blood gush from every last pore in your body. The pain and suffering are unbearable and you long to escape.

In the Wailing Hell, you find yourself inside an iron building and the doors are sealed shut. Fire blazes from all directions, incinerating your body until there is nothing left but ash. Realizing there is no escape, you let out a mournful cry. You are stuffed into another iron building, which is enclosed by the first, the Howling Hell. Realizing that even if you were to get out of the first building, you would still not be able to get out of the second one, you experience twice as much suffering as before. Your plight is extremely wretched.

In the Inferno, you are impaled with a blazing iron stake through the anus all the way to the crown of your head. Red tongues of fire blaze from all of your sense gates. At times your whole body is submerged in a cauldron of molten metal, and you are tortured as your flesh melts off your bones.

In the Great Inferno, you are impaled with a trident. The center prong stabs straight through the crown of your head, and the other two prongs pierce your right and left shoulders. A sheet of burning iron is wrapped around you like a blanket, and your flesh is cooked raw in boiling molten metal. This causes your skin and flesh to come off, until nothing is left but a skeleton. Born as a being in this realm, your suffering is a hundred times more intense than what you experienced before. The unbearable pain causes you to let out a whole range of piercing cries and screams as you long to escape.

The Hell of Incessant Torment is an infinite, boundless expanse of incredibly hot, blazing flames that incinerate your body so completely that it is no longer distinguishable from the fire. Aside from the intense screams that can be heard, physical bodies cannot even be seen there. The suffering is unbearable, and intense and anguished cries are heard throughout.

As you envision all this, the King of Great Bliss from Oddiyana appears in the sky before you. "Alas, you unfortunate being!" he says, "You have accumulated a tremendous amount of karma spurred on by your own anger. The violent anger you directed toward a particular object has resulted in the suffering you now experience in these hells. Now, confess your nonvirtuous acts with intense regret and cultivate great compassion for all the sentient beings in a similar plight. If you arouse the courage to take on the suffering of others, you may be able to free yourself!

"Long ago, Shakyamuni was born as the strongman Pakshita in hell, where he had to pull a wagon. His companion at the time, Kamarupa, aroused the wrath of the guards by not doing his share of the work. The enraged guards beat him on the head with iron hammers. Seeing this, Shakyamuni felt boundless compassion for his friend. The wish to trade his own happiness for the suffering of another was born in his mind.

"'Please put the rope of his wagon around my neck,' he asked.

"The guardians of hell, however, responded by saying, 'Who can experience the karma of another?' and began beating him on the head with a hammer. He died in an instant, only to be reborn in the Heaven of the Thirty-Three, where he was liberated from his suffering."

Hearing this story, you arouse bodhichitta and think: "Even if I have to stay here I will bear it so long as the other sentient beings like me are liberated from this suffering!" As soon as you generate this intention, a hook-like ray of white light bursts forth from the heart center of the Great Master of Oddiyana. The two of you merge inseparably and you attain buddhahood, endowed with the ability to accomplish both your own and others' benefit spontaneously. Next, imagine that a similar light emanates from your own heart center, instantly summoning all sentient beings and emptying the realms of hell.

As an aside, the life spans of the beings in these hells are enumerated in general sutras such as the *Application of Mindfulness Sutra*, *The Delineation of Karma*, and the *Treasury of Higher Dharma*. It is also explained, however, that in the context of the application of these antidotes, there is no fixed life span. The great Omniscient One wrote:

> It is taught that when a powerful antidote takes root in one's mind or something similar occurs, transference can take place suddenly, whereas despising one's vajra master and other such actions can necessitate remaining [in a particular state] for many great eons. Hence, the delineation is made in terms of karmic obscuration.

This topic can also be understood from the story of strongman Pakshita that was told earlier, the tale of Dzawo's daughter, and so on.

The Eight Cold Hells

Envision yourself in a strange land where the ground is a vast desert of burning sand and there isn't even a slight, cool breeze. Tortured by the heat of the sun, you grow exhausted, yet you continue on in a vacant stupor. "If only it were just a bit cooler than this," you think.

This thought stops the experience of intense heat, and you are instantly reborn in the eight cold hells. The entire ground is an expanse of snow, and the canyons and ravines are filled with solid ice. You are surrounded in all directions by massive snow mountains. A blizzard swirls above, plunging the area into dense darkness. An icy wind howls. In the midst of this is the Hell of Blisters, where the driving snow and wind pierce your body and you instantly break out in unbearable blisters. As your skin and flesh contract, your unbearable suffering produces a state of intense terror. The blisters on your body then burst open and blood and pus gush out. Your suffering worsens, and you scream out of desperation. The suffering grows greater still and the strength of your voice breaks, until nothing but a faint groan comes out, and then the suffering grows even more intense until no sound at all comes out, save the chattering of your teeth. You are hit by a gale-force wind that causes you to turn a clear bluish color and makes your skin split open into six small cracks, like the petals of an utpala flower. The skin is peeled off by the piercing cold and the blood-red flesh splits into ten pieces like the petals of a lotus. The cracks increase and grow wider, like a lotus in full bloom, and you experience suffering that is a hundred times greater than before.

If you filled a container with eighty Magadha measures of sesame seeds and then removed one grain every hundred years, the length of time it would take for the seeds to run out is said to be equal to the life span of those in the Hell of Blisters. Meditate on this understanding until you become extremely dejected and disheartened.

Once again, your root guru appears in the sky before you in the form of the Great Master of Oddiyana. "Child," he says, "understand that your suffering is karma, and rejoice that it is being exhausted. With a feeling of intense compassion, take on still more to relieve the suffering of others, using this extraordinary antidote!"

Just hearing this triggers bodhichitta to arise, and you think to yourself, "How terribly sad. Just think of all the other sentient beings who suffer in the cold hells just like me. Even if I have to endure suffering a hundred thousand times greater than this, I will bear it if it means that I will be able to experience the fate of these beings for them. May all these beings be freed from their suffering!"

When you think this, your bad karma is instantly exhausted. You are swiftly transferred to the heart center of the Great Master of Oddiyana, where you become a realized guide capable of leading beings. Next, simply observe the true nature of the pleasurable and painful experiences that arise and let your consciousness rest naturally.

THE SUFFERING OF SPIRITS

Letter to a Friend states:

> Spirits undergo an unending stream of suffering
> Brought on by their unfulfilled desires.
> Hunger, thirst, cold, heat, fatigue, and fear
> Make their experience unbearable.

There are said to be three types of spirits. To create an approximate subjective experience of the suffering they encounter, imagine feeling an intense craving for food, clothing, and material things. This creates a feeling of stinginess when you make offerings and serve extraordinary individuals, causing you to be reborn instantly as a spirit with external obscurations. Your desire to enjoy fruits, rivers, and so on, drives you to travel great distances. Weary with fatigue, you arrive, only to find that the things and places you seek are either guarded by weapon-wielding creatures or transformed into pus, blood, and other foul substances. You feel utterly chagrined, in addition to suffering unbearably from hunger and thirst.

Those with internal obscurations suffer from not finding anything to eat or drink for months and years on end. They live in a city called Kapilavastu, a fearful desert devoid of water, vegetation, and other desirable things. Even when these beings manage to find some form of sustenance, they are unable to get it inside their mouths, which are as tiny as the eye of a needle. When a little bit does fit in, it can't pass through their throats, which are as narrow as the hair of a horse's tail. Even if some does make it down, it will never fill them up, as their stomachs are as big as Mount Meru. Their limbs are as thin as grass blades and cannot support their weight. These and other sufferings comprise the extremely wretched plight of these beings.

Next are the spirits with obscurations related to food and drink. When food or drink enters their stomachs, it bursts into flames and incinerates their bodies. They are so wretched that they eat their own flesh and consume excrement and urine. Their experience of heat and cold is dysfunctional as well. In the warmth of summer, even the cool sensation of the moon makes them hot, and in the biting cold of winter, even the sun's rays feel cool to them. Just looking at rivers and the like causes them to dry up and manifest as inhospitable ravines. They experience an incalculable number of sufferings due to hunger and thirst. Moreover, it is not enough for these sufferings to last only a short time: they must endure them for fifteen thousand human years.

Knowing this, meditate until you feel sad and dejected. Once more, your root guru appears in the sky before you in the form of the Great Master of Oddiyana. "Oh, all this suffering that has unerringly befallen you is due to your own stinginess. It will be difficult for even the buddhas of the three times to protect you now! Just as victorious Shakyamuni taught King Bimbisara, you must own your own karma and rejoice that your negative karma is being exhausted. With a feeling of compassion toward sentient beings who are suffering in situations similar to your own, cultivate the courage to take on their suffering in addition to your own and utilize this antidote!"

Just hearing these words makes you cry out in sadness, "Alas! Up until now, these sentient beings have been wandering throughout the boundless reaches of samsara in a state of desperate clinging, just like me, and experiencing sufferings such as these. Spirits just like me are as numerous as the number of grains of sand in the River Ganges, and they all experience nothing but this suffering. How terribly sad!

I will now bear my own suffering and readily take on the suffering of others. May this city of spirits be emptied to its very foundations!"

Imagine that the moment you think this, your negative karma is instantly exhausted and you attain buddhahood, merging inseparably with the wisdom mind of the Great Master of Oddiyana. These sentient beings, as well, are drawn out of their suffering by the light rays from your heart center. Finally, examine what it is that moves and what it is that is still.

In addition to the hells mentioned above, the Vinaya scriptures state:

> Then Maudgalyayana crossed over the oceans and saw the sentient beings of the Ephemeral Hells being born as pestles, brooms, and trees, and being tormented by a great many sufferings.

The Neighboring Hells are situated in the midst of the two groups of eight [Hot and Cold Hells]. The individual locations of the Ephemeral and Neighboring Hells are explained in the *Treasury of the Supreme Vehicle*:

> The location of the Ephemeral Hells is not fixed, as they can be found in various places: the earth, water, fire, and air.
> The Neighboring Hells are located in the immediate environs of the two groups of eight.

Thus, these two are grouped into one category.

Concerning the spirits discussed above, the Great Omniscient One taught:

> There are terrestrial and celestial spirits. . . .

Of the divisions mentioned here, terrestrial spirits are the three groups discussed previously. Celestial spirits, or minor spirits, are mentioned in the root verses of the *Great Chariot*:

The spirits that move in space are ghosts, demons,
  harm-bringers,
Flesh-eaters, powerful ghosts, the king-spirits, and
  others.

One should know how to use these and other passages to give a more elaborate presentation to those with the sharpest faculties,[2] while for others the standard presentation will suffice.

THE SUFFERING OF ANIMALS

Letter to a Friend states:

Those born as animals are killed, bound, and beaten;
They experience all manner of suffering.
Those who abandon the virtue that brings peace
Will end up eating one another, an intolerable state.

Animals are classified into two categories: those that live in the depths and those that are scattered elsewhere. The following contemplation related to the suffering of these two groups stems from the *Treatise on the Levels*. Imagine that your afflicted mental state is one of dense ignorance, which causes you to be instantaneously reborn as a creature living in the depths of a vast ocean. The waters of this ocean are teeming with fish, mollusks, sea monsters, and so forth, all crowded together like the dregs left over from fermented beer. At times, you are bigger than the other fish, and the smaller creatures bore into your body; this feels as painful as an arrow piercing your heart. At other times, you are smaller, and the bigger fish swallow you, causing you to suffer as though your body were being stuffed into a small iron box. When you find yourself between the iron mountains that lie at the edge of this and other continents, where neither the sun nor the moon shines, it is so dark that you cannot even see your own arm when it is stretched out before you. All this makes you suffer.

Animals that are scattered elsewhere include birds, hoofed herbivores, insects, and other wild animals. Those that are undomesticated suffer from being out in nature, where they endure heat, cold, hunger, and thirst, and where they prey upon one another.

Hence, this very evening, or even right now, such creatures may find themselves at the juncture between this life and the next. This can happen in the time it takes to snap your fingers. All the people and other beings you see are perceived as bloodthirsty executioners who want to kill you with their bare hands. All appearances seem suspicious. You are on guard even when taking a bite of food, keeping watch in all directions. In particular, you are in danger of being killed in an instant by one of the merciless methods used by hunters and fishermen.

Domesticated animals, on the other hand, such as horses, yaks, goats, sheep, cattle, and so forth, are all tortured by having an iron bit put in their mouths and being ridden long distances. Some are flipped onto their backs, the soft, warm part of their underbellies sliced open with a sharp knife, their stomachs torn out, and their life force severed. Others have their noses pierced and are castrated, beaten, bled, and loaded to capacity.

Nagas, as well, suffer from things such as burning sand, the fear of garudas, vidya mantras, and being abandoned, outcast, and friendless.

Animals share such common sufferings as ignorance and having no fixed life span. Also, by their very nature, all of these animals lack the ability to distinguish right from wrong.

Contemplate the specific sufferings found in each of these realms until the mere thought of samsara makes you sick. The Omniscient One wrote:

> Having contemplated their plight, in order to bring well-
> being and happiness
> To those seeking freedom from the animal world,
> Establish them on the sublime path of higher rebirths and
> liberation
> By diligently practicing virtue night and day.

After experiencing this series of sufferings for yourself, conclude by imagining that you are reborn as a naga and that a garuda carries you up into the sky.

"Each breath could be my last! I am now at the juncture between this life and the next," you cry out, "How terrifying! I'm being eaten alive by this frightful, powerful bird! Oh no! Oh no!" As you scream in terror, the taste of true fear overwhelms you and you lose consciousness.

Once again, your root guru appears in the sky above you, taking the form of the Great Master of Oddiyana. "Alas, you unfortunate being," he says. "Even though you are forced to endure this kind of suffering and terror, you have poured all your energy into perpetuating the endless samsara of self-cherishing, and this is the result. Now, if you meditate upon extraordinary bodhichitta and cherish others more than yourself, you can free yourself from all this.

"Long ago, when the Lion of the Shakyas, Lord of the Teachings, was training in the conduct of the bodhisattva, he was born as the son of Vallabha, with the name "Daughter." Ignoring the words of his mother, Daughter kicked his mother in the head and went to sea in search of precious gems. After some time, however, his ship was wrecked. Holding on to a piece of wood, he ended up on an island.

"He eventually reached an iron house. Inside, there was a person whose head was being cut open by a revolving steel wheel that bore into his brain.

"'What did this person do?' he inquired.

"'This is the fully ripened karmic effect of kicking his mother in the head,' came the reply.

"'Well then, I too was led here by my karma,' he thought.

"Then a voice came from the sky, 'Let those who are bound be freed, and those who are free be bound!' The disc was suddenly spinning on his own head, causing him unbearable suffering.

"The pain awakened in him a feeling of intense compassion for all the sentient beings in the same state as himself. 'How sad! There must be many other beings experiencing such suffering! May their negativity and suffering come to me instead!'

"The moment he thought this the wheel flew up into the sky and he was freed from his suffering. Therefore, the wish to put others before yourself is extremely powerful, so cultivate great compassion for all the infinite number of sentient beings who suffer as you do. Take on their sufferings in addition to your own and rejoice!"

Just hearing this causes you to generate an intense feeling of compassion for all the sentient beings in situations similar to your own. This, coupled with the courage that you now have to give away your own happiness and take on the suffering of others, instantly purifies your negative karma. Your fear, like an unreal appearance in a dream, then vanishes; you merge inseparably with the Great Master of Oddiyana and attain buddhahood. Visualize yourself emanating light rays to all the different animal species and imagine that they are drawn up to the ranks of the four kinds of masters of awareness, like a flock of birds startled by the stone from a slingshot. Finally, cut through the flow of discursive thought and allow your mindfulness and awareness to relax without restriction.

DISSATISFACTION IN THE HIGHER REALMS

At this point, you may think that rebirth in the three lower realms fits these descriptions but that the attainment of the higher realms offers no such suffering, and grants only happiness. This, however, is not the case. *Letter to a Friend* explains:

> Even the great happiness experienced in the higher realms
> Is outweighed by the suffering of death and transmigration.

And:

> When transmigrating from the heavens,
> Those who have no virtue left are powerless;
> They will end up in the animal, spirit,
> Or hell realms, whatever the case may be.

While the *Application of Mindfulness Sutra* teaches:

> Humans are impaired by a short life span.
> Gods are impaired by their own carelessness.
> Demigods are impaired by quarreling and strife.
> There is no happiness to be had in samsara,
> Not even so much as a needle tip's worth!

Even if you manage to attain a pleasurable human existence in the higher realms, overt experiences of suffering will soon pile up, like what you might experience if your mother were to pass away right after your father. With the suffering of change, what seems pleasant one moment can suddenly change to suffering, like being killed instantly by eating poisoned food or drowning while swimming across a river for fun. The pervasive suffering of conditioning is the result of conditioning factors, such as experiencing a serious illness due to improper diet, clothing, or behavior, or the retribution one might experience after attacking a powerful individual. These are the three root sufferings. The Vinaya scriptures state:

> Samsara is a heap of suffering.
> The suffering of suffering, of conditioning,
> And of change—these three and the eight
> Bring intense suffering to humans.

In addition to the three root sufferings, humans also suffer terribly from being afflicted by the eight subsidiary sufferings: the four sufferings of birth, old age, sickness, and death, as well as meeting with hated enemies, being separated from loved ones, being bereft of the objects of one's desires, and the continual perception of suffering due to the five perpetuating aggregates. For this reason, the Great Omniscient One writes:

> Hence, all of human existence is devoid of happiness,
> Due to the causes and results of suffering.
> To liberate yourself from this, contemplate the excellent
> Dharma
> And employ methods that bring liberation from samsara's
> realms.

Similarly, there is incalculable suffering in the heavens of the desire-realm gods. Although the Heaven of the Four Great Kings [50], the Heaven of the Thirty-Three [100], the Heaven of Gemini [200], the Joyous Heaven [400], the Heaven of Enjoyable Manifestations [800], and the Heaven of Mastery over Others' Creations [1600] do appear to be pleasurable states,[3] in fact, the beings there experience nothing but the grievous sufferings of change and conditioning. When they die, their skin turns an ugly hue, their flower garlands wither, they grow depressed, their divine spouses leave them, and their thoughts become disturbed. When they perceive their future birthplaces with their divine eyes, what they see causes them to panic and faint. Their divine mothers and fathers, friends, loved ones, and so forth cry out from afar: "May you be reborn as a human in Jambudvipa! May you practice the ten virtues and be born here in the heavens once again!" With these wishes and aspirations, they scatter flowers and run far away. They undergo these sufferings for seven of the god-realm days. How wretched! When we humans die, our friends and family gather around our beds and do whatever they can to please us, yet we still suffer horribly and fall into great despair. So it should go without saying how much the gods suffer from death and transmigration.

Furthermore, the magnificent form-realm gods of meditative absorption also die. This includes those in the Heaven of the Class of Brahma up to those in the Heaven of Great Result. When these gods pass away, the pleasure they experience in the present transforms and they experience the incalculable suffering of entering into the next state of existence. Noble Nagarjuna explains:

> Even those in the Abode of Brahma and all the other
>   spontaneously accomplished absorptions,
> Who seem so majestically radiant and beautiful,
> Fail to apprehend their dormant concept of self,
> So is there any way to be sure that they won't be reborn
>   in hell once they die?

Similarly, the four formless realms are not proximate causes of omniscience. Rather, they are neutral states of absorption that are ephemeral and diffuse planes of existence. Just as a bird flying in the sky must eventually land on solid ground, at some point these beings will have to die, transmigrate, and experience the indeterminate sufferings of their next existence. What a mistake it is to place one's trust in such ephemeral forms of happiness! *Letter to a Student* states:

> In this world, terrorized as it is by a flaming mass of
> suffering,
> Those who arrogantly take suffering to be happiness
> Invite the jaws of the Lord of Death to open once again,
> For this is the seed of the tree of their future births.

Furthermore, the suffering of demigods is even more intense. *Letter to a Friend* states:

> The natural animosity that demigods feel toward the glory
> of the gods
> Greatly pains their minds.
> Though they may be intelligent, the obscurations of these
> beings
> Prevents them from seeing the truth.

When demigods see the happiness and wealth of the gods in the Heaven of the Thirty-Three, they burn with the fire of hatred and jealousy. This drives them to wage war with the gods. The suffering they undergo on the battlefield is agonizing: their heads and limbs are severed by vajras, arrows, discs, and other weapons; their life force ceases; their bodies are severely injured; and they end up meeting their own death. Even if they happen to be intelligent, they will not attain the path of seeing of the listeners due to the influence of obscurations. Consequently, it is said that they do not see the truth.

Citing the *Heap of Jewels Sutra*, however, the Great Omniscient One wrote that this is not the case according to the Great Vehicle. Regardless, it is necessary to exert yourself in the means for avoiding such states of existence. On this point, the Omniscient One writes:

> As the demigods suffer terribly,
> Then those beings with peaceful, virtuous karma
> Must swiftly set out to practice the sacred Dharma!

Thus, the suffering of samsara is boundless and severely oppressive. No sooner are you freed from one painful experience than you get caught up in another, like a bucket spinning around on a water wheel or a bee caught in a jar. By its very nature, samsara is nothing but suffering. As the *Letter to a Student* states:

> The one who, revolving through the perpetual cycle
>   of samsara,
> Views a moment's respite as happiness,
> Is sure to wander in the forms of all kinds of beings
> Powerlessly over hundreds [of lifetimes].

You may think: "Well, I'm not too worried. The Buddha will protect me from the lower realms and all the sufferings commonly experienced by the six classes of beings." But this isn't the case. The Vinaya quotes the Buddha as saying:

> I have shown you the path to liberation,
> But liberation depends on you, so be diligent!

Since we are confused about what we should and shouldn't do, the Blissful One used various means to show us the path to liberation. However, just as no one has the power to stop us from dreaming when we are in a deep slumber, actual liberation from samsara and the lower realms depends solely on our own diligence. We can be sure that if this were not the case, one of the compassionate buddhas would have emptied existence long ago with his or her light rays of compassion.

We have fallen into the pit of samsara and are bound tight by the shackles of dualistic perception. Stabbed by the blades of the afflictions, we are enduring the suffering of the present, and we have no choice but to be led to more suffering in the future. Think this over well and cultivate infinite compassion for all the six classes of sentient beings. To lead them all to the path of liberation, from this day forward in whatever ways you can, make offerings to the Three Jewels, the source of all sublime qualities. If you harbor a nonvirtuous thought for even an instant, use a strong antidote to subdue it, and then confess and vow to avoid such negativity in the future. The Vinaya scriptures explain:

> Do not take small negative acts lightly,
> Believing they can do no harm,
> For even a tiny spark
> Can burn a mountain of grass.

You should amass virtuous thoughts, even those that seem insignificant, and pass your time doing only what is wholesome and virtuous. Some claim that they are unable to study and contemplate because they have limited intelligence. Others claim that they cannot make offerings or gifts of material wealth because they are not rich enough. Still others claim that they are simply too old for Dharma practice to be effective. Although people make all kinds of excuses, it is mainly their own mind that is holding them back. The teachings say that even an animal can attain liberation if it can arouse diligence and confidence, so why even mention that this is true for humans? As Shantideva once wrote:

> Do not let yourself be discouraged,
> Thinking, "How could enlightenment be for me?"
> This the Thus-Gone rightly said,
> And thus these true words were spoken.

> Even flies, mosquitoes, bees, and worms
> Could reach unsurpassed enlightenment,
> Difficult to attain though it may be,
> Were they to muster the strength of diligence.

> What, then, of a human being like me?
> I recognize what is beneficial and what harms,
> So if I don't reject enlightened conduct
> Why should I not be able to attain enlightenment?

And in the *Ornament of the Sutras*:

> Since limitless human beings
> Attain perfect enlightenment
> In each and every moment,
> Do not be discouraged.

On the other hand, no matter how much virtuous karma you have, avoid becoming satisfied with yourself or trying to calculate how much you have. As the *Flower Ornament Sutra* states:

> Noble child, do not become attached to one virtuous deed. Do not be satisfied with perfecting one approach to the Dharma or one activity. "Why?" you may ask. Because, noble child, a bodhisattva must amass an infinite number of virtuous deeds.

However much we strive toward virtue, a close investigation will reveal that our "virtue" is mixed with negativity and nonvirtue. While an occasional pure act of virtue may be possible, the vast majority of sentient beings have impure perception, so it is exceedingly rare to accumulate virtuous deeds that are embraced by the threefold excellence: the excellent preparation, main practice, and conclusion. Therefore, when it comes to the virtue linked with merit that runs out after a single ripening, you may boast of having as much as the supreme central mountain (that is, Mount Meru), but this virtue is as insubstantial as an autumn cloud. So even if you are just considering stretching out your arm, always make sure that it becomes a pure act of virtue.

The Guru

The *Child Scripture* states:

> Think to yourself, "I must receive the essential instructions of my guru at all costs. I must do whatever it takes to receive them!"

There is not even a needle's tip worth of happiness to be had in the six realms; there is nothing but suffering. But once you've understood this, just getting depressed about it won't free you from suffering. You need to devote yourself solely to the methods that will help the situation. And what are these methods? The *Sutra of Advice to King Prasenajid* explains:

> At that time, Great King, you will have no refuge or protection aside from the sacred Dharma. At that time, the sacred Dharma will be your refuge and protection, your support, sanctuary, and defender.

This is not just a matter of reading books. Just as butter comes from milk and smoke from fire, you will be able to grasp the essence only by serving a teacher, the root of the path. As stated in the *Compendium*:

> Always serve gurus who are learned,
> Because the qualities of learnedness come from such gurus.

Just as patients rely upon their doctors to be cured,
Do not be careless when it comes to serving a guru.

Concerning the qualifications a guru should have, the *Heap of Jewels Sutra* states:

"How should one serve a teacher?" Maitreya asked.
"Think of each and every teaching that your teacher gives," the Buddha replied, "as nothing other than the ultimate truth, the sphere of reality itself. These teachings and clarifications are [the teacher's way] of leading you straight along the path."

On the basis of this passage, the *Ornament of the Sutras* teaches that a guru's mind should be thoroughly tamed by the three higher trainings, and that a guru should have studied widely and without any partiality, and thus possess the quality of scriptural transmission. The guru should have the quality of special superiority, in the sense that his or her training in the sublime knowledge of realizing the basic nature makes the guru superior to the students. A guru needs to be aware of the underlying intent of the scriptures and be able to use the sublime strength of his or her discernment to present them in ways that disciples find pleasing, thereby leading them to the ultimate path. A guru should be unconcerned with wealth and honor and be loving and compassionate toward those who are less fortunate. Finally, a guru should not get tired of having to explain things repeatedly and have the strength of character to tolerate ingratitude.

According to the *General Sutra That Embodies All Intents*, gurus can also be divided into the following categories:

Gurus fall into one of the following categories: the outer guru who is skilled in cutting through misconceptions, the kind inner guru who teaches the instructions of the Secret Mantra, the secret root guru who points out the nonarising nature of mind and shows the mind's essence to be birthless, the natural guru of the ground, the guru

of your own mind's purity, the guru of symbolic appearances, and lineage gurus.

As an aside, the qualifications of the student are discussed in the
Tantra of the Clear Expanse:

> Students who are unworthy vessels
> Are unintelligent, flattering, and insincere.
> These tight-fisted, sweet-talking hypocrites
> Are thankless and break the guru's command.
> They don't see good qualities, and instead examine faults.
> Both their ancestry and mind-stream are base,
> And they belittle the kindness of others, only to praise
> themselves.
> They are lax when it comes to vows, samaya, and practice.[1]
> Failure to examine the student is the enemy of the master.

One should begin by checking for the traits listed here.

As for the qualities of the student who should be taught, the
Luminous Tantra of Self-Manifesting Awareness states:

> Strong faith and great diligence,
> Great intelligence and no attachment,
> Great reverence and Secret Mantra conduct,
> Nonconceptuality and an undistracted mind,
> With samaya vows and diligence in practice . . .

The teachings should not be given to anyone who lacks the qualities
mentioned here.

If such a master and student come together, there will be that
much less difficulty in accomplishing enlightenment, just as a bird
with two wings flies easily through the sky. Therefore, students need
to serve a qualified guru as well. They should look for any flaws and
defects that conflict with the teachings, immediately recognize what
is the most dominant, and then apply the appropriate remedy to
their mind-stream.

I. Serving a Teacher in Thought

Next comes the actual practice of serving a teacher, of which there are two forms: serving a teacher in thought and serving a teacher in deed. The first of these is explained in the *Dharani of the Jewel Lamp*:

> Developing faith is the prerequisite, like a mother.
> It safeguards all positive qualities and causes them to develop.
> It clears away doubt and delivers one from the rivers [of suffering].
> Faith characterizes the city of happiness and goodness.
> Faith clears away impurities and clarifies the mind.
> It eliminates pride and is the root of respect.
> Faith is the supreme wealth, treasure, and support.
> Like a hand, it is the root of gathering virtue.

As shown here, it is absolutely necessary to avoid treating one's teacher as an equal and to have heartfelt, unshakable faith, just as noble Sadaprarudita did when he observed the enlightened qualities of the bodhisattva Dharmodgata.[2]

Our own impure karma may cause us to misperceive the acts of our gurus, even those who are fully qualified. We miss the point that they are trying to convey with the various activities they perform, those that are provisional, definitive, covert, and intentional, and they appear to us as having a mixture of faults and virtues. When this occurs, we need to stop our judgmental thoughts. If we can stop them, it is only natural that we will automatically perceive everything the guru does as sublime.

Therefore, all our misperceptions of the guru's activities need to be consciously addressed and remedied in the following way: If a negative thought suddenly arises concerning the goodness or badness of the guru's behavior, the way he or she imparts advice, or even about something as insignificant as the way he or she dresses, you should address it as soon as it manifests and avoid pursuing such ego-fixation. Rather, think to yourself, "It is impossible for a miserable being like me to say that such an extraordinary guru like this has these faults and shortcomings! It is the strength of my own habitual karma and afflictions from time immemorial that makes the guru seem flawed. What difference is there between this and the strands of hair falling from the sky that are seen by an old woman who eats henbane, or a conch appearing yellow to someone afflicted with jaundice? How can I be sure that the guru isn't displaying these impure activities on purpose, in ways that intentionally correspond to my own behavior, my heart pierced as it is by the five arrows of desire? Even the Supreme Guide Shakyamuni, who completely rid himself of all shortcomings and perfected all positive qualities, was perceived as a mass of faults by the monk Sunakshatra, Devadatta, the six Hindu teachers, and other individuals. Likewise, the bodhisattvas of the past—the learned and accomplished abbot Shantarakshita, the master Padmasambhava, King Trisong Deutsen, and his ministers—were seen as criminals by the Bönpos and evil, hostile ministers. This is no different than what happened with noble Asanga, who saw the Invincible Protector Maitreya as a dog whose hind quarters were crawling with maggots.[3] According to the *Meeting of Father and Son Sutra*, the Blissful One even took the form of a demon to work for the welfare of sentient beings, so seeing the Buddha as a demon is only my own impure perception; objectively speaking, there never were any flaws." You should generate certainty about this and think it through, over and over, for this will enable you to overpower the misconceptions of the one who sees faults.

It is stated in the *Summarized Meaning of the Tantras*:

> Regard all the guru's actions
> As the actions of a buddha.
> View his sleeping or rising
> As the illusory appearance of luminosity.
> Even his prostrations and circumambulations
> Show the very expression of buddhahood.
> When he dances or shows some expression,
> It is the intentional act of a buddha.
> Whether he appears angry or impassioned,

Regard him as an enlightened buddha.
Even if he kills a hundred people at once,
It is the work of a buddha to benefit beings.
Even if he enjoys a hundred queens,
It is mahamudra, the wisdom of great bliss.
Whatever wishes and ambitions may appear
Are free from desire, the state of buddhahood;
All are the acts of a buddha.
Whatever you see him do is the path of excellence,
Whatever you hear him say is the sacred Dharma,
Whatever he thinks is the glory of omniscience.
For a guru to be confused is virtually impossible.
Since it won't happen,
If what you perceive appears to be confusion,
This is your own perception, your own impure mind,
Just as one who is visually impaired
Manifestly perceives snow to be black,
Though it is impossible for snow ever to be black;
Just as a jaundiced person
Perceives a conch to be yellow,
Though it is actually always white;
And just as one with perverted desires
May see water as pus, blood, and weapons,
Though no pus, blood, and weapons are there.
Therefore, if misperceptions arise concerning the guru's
  liberated life,
The path to liberation will be blocked.
Since the guru is acting skillfully to tame beings,
Know that his or her actions are symbolic and skillful
  methods.

Hence, in terms of the definitive truth, such enlightened beings have
been free of fault from the very beginning. Once you feel sure of this
from the very core of your being, all excellent qualities will occur
quite spontaneously. On this point, the master Nagarjuna wrote:

If someone were to fall from the peak of Mount Meru,
Even if that person were to think he was not falling, he still
    falls.
Once you have received beneficial transmissions through
    the guru's kindness,
While you may think that you are not becoming liberated,
    you are.

To generate great respect, you need to see even a rebuke as a
Dharma teaching, and even if the guru hits or beats you, you need to
see it as a blessing. The scriptural divisions explain:

In brief, beatings and scoldings,
Wrathful mantras, doing battle, stabbing and hitting with
    weapons,
Whatever the guru does, it is only a method
To eliminate one's defilement of faults.
Disrespect toward the guru should be relinquished.
The acts of enlightened body, speech, and mind
Are all the miraculous display of
The dance of a buddha.
Do not think of them in any other way.
If you do, you will have turned your back on spiritual
    attainments.
To lose devotion is to be in Mara's grasp;
You will have many illnesses, a short life, and you will fall to
    the lower realms.

Thus, in light of this, your guru, who has exhausted all faults and
perfected every enlightened quality, is no different than the consum-
mately purified and realized buddhas. Nevertheless, your inferior
merit and karma prevent you from accurately perceiving the appearance aspect of the guru's three kayas, which is why the guru manifests
in an ordinary way. As is written in the *Gathering of the Masters of
Awareness Tantra*:

The buddhas and their heirs
Manifest in forms
That match their disciples.

Furthermore, the inner clarity of the dharmakaya buddha, the youthful vase body, is ennobled by six unique qualities relative to the all-ground. This primordial protector is beheld by the wisdom of consummate purification and realization; it is not within the experiential range of anyone else. The sambhogakaya is endowed with the five certainties and the seven aspects of union. It does not appear to anyone other than those extraordinary disciples who have mastered the ten grounds. A nirmanakaya buddha has mastery over the ten strengths, the fourfold fearlessness, and so forth. This is the teacher of the listeners and solitary buddhas.

Other beings are bereft of the merit required to receive the kindness of a nirmanakaya buddha. It is not that those who manifest the three kayas are biased and have intentionally spurned us. Rather, it is our own inferior karma and circumstances that prevent us from meeting those buddhas and becoming a fit vessel to receive their teachings, just as the sun doesn't shine on a north-facing cave. The fact that you have fallen into the boundless dungeon of samsara and have been here as long as you have comes down to nothing more than this.

That said, to have obtained a human existence and met with an enlightened teacher is extremely fortunate. It is said in many sutras and tantras that the buddhas will emanate as masters that take the form of ordinary people in order to benefit those of us who find ourselves in the final five hundred years [of this fortunate eon]. This is how they will tame their disciples. Thus, your enlightened guru as well is no ordinary person in terms of the definitive truth. From your perspective, your guru is superior even to the Buddha, since he or she is the one who has actually taught you the instructions. Even if you were to meet the Buddha face to face, adorned as he is with the major and minor marks, there isn't anything he could do that would be greater than teaching you the vast and profound sacred Dharma and leading you to the state of liberation and omniscience. Therefore, if you are able to put into practice the meaning [of what you learned while] properly serving a teacher, have no doubt that you will attain the states of the higher realms and definite goodness.

If you regard those who give you ordinary food and clothing or protect you from enemies and malevolent forces in this present life as extremely kind, then how could you possibly repay the kindness of the guru who dispels the suffering of boundless samsara and brings you to a lasting state of happiness, even if you filled the mighty golden base of the universe with gold from the Jambu River? This is why, from your perspective as a disciple, your own enlightened gurus are kinder than all the buddhas and are, in this sense, superior to them. Keeping this in mind, you should cultivate faith, respect, and devotion from the very core of your heart. As the *Mother Tantra of the Clear Expanse* says:

> The supreme physician, pacifying illness and negative
>   forces,
> A precious jewel, satisfying needs and desires,
> An elixir, bringing everything under its sway,
> A vessel, liberating all beings without exception,
> Supreme sovereign of all enlightened activity,
> The guru is paramount!
> For those attached to samsara
> The primary method for reversing fixation is the guru.
> For those who fail to remember the sacred Dharma,
> And who recognize neither virtue nor vice,
> The enlightened guru, who teaches the Dharma and distin-
>   guishes virtue from vice,
> Should be held in the highest esteem.
> For those enveloped by obstacles that inhibit meditation,
> The elimination of obstacles and the results that ensue
> Arise from the kindness of the gurus.

And:

> All Dharmas, both of cause and result,
> Come from the mouth of the guru.

All buddhas of the three times as well,
Come from following a guru.

Therefore, once you have met a qualified enlightened guru, one who is not evil or deceitful, devotion should arise such that you see whatever the guru does as sublime. This faith that comes from deep within is a sign that you have received the guru's blessings. Artificial devotion, on the other hand, will result in an unstable faith, and the slightest appearance of impure behavior will undermine it. For this reason, this sort of faith is unreliable.

II. SERVING A TEACHER IN DEED

Serving a guru in deed involves guarding three sets of ten samaya vows related to body, speech, and mind, along with their subsidiaries. The *Tantra of the Self-Occurring and Self-Arisen* states:

> First, the samayas of enlightened form—
> First are the ten to be observed physically:
> Do not walk in front of the guru,
> Because it will be as though you have scornfully turned
>   your back on the guru,
> And you will be born in the animal realm where there is
>   no Dharma.
>
> Do not walk behind the guru,
> Because you will tread on his or her footsteps,
> And you will be born without protector or refuge.
>
> Do not walk to the right of the guru,
> Because it will seem as though you are attacking,
> And you will have a short life, many illnesses, and will
>   fall to hell.
>
> Do not tread on the shadow of the guru's head,
> Because this is a sign of contempt,
> And you will fall into the Howling Hell.

Do not tread on the guru's hair,
Because this is like insulting a buddha,
And you will be born in the hell where black lines are
    drawn.

Do not tread on the guru's pillow or seat,
Because it is like criticizing the unsurpassable Buddha,
And you will be born as one who climbs the Hill of Shalma
    Trees.

Do not measure the guru's height,
Because it will be as though you have hit him or her with
    your hand,
And you will be vanquished with three hundred spears.

Do not take the guru's cane,
As this obstructs the outset of the path to liberation and
    the higher realms,
And you will be born in the Hell of Mental Blankness.

If you listen to even three words of the guru's
Profound key instructions, you are not to take a higher
    place,
As you will slip into the mire of misguided knowledge.

If you divvy up your belongings or food
Without offering the best to your guru,
You will be reborn in a body of blazing flesh and blood.

Furthermore, if you stay seated when she or he arises,
You will be reborn in a hell with your head separated from
    your body.
If you sit elevated when the guru is seated,
You will be born in hell with a drooping head.

These are the ten physical samayas.
If they degenerate, for one great eon

You will be born in karmic hot and cold hells.
To rectify impairments, build a stupa
And place images of the guru in its center.
Making offerings and circumambulate it unceasingly.

And:

Verbally, observe these ten samayas:
The guru is superior to all the buddhas.
It is not appropriate to say all sorts of things to him or her.
Speaking derisively behind the back of the guru
Is to turn one's back on the Buddha.
With no fruition, one will fall to the lower realms
With a rotted body, a blocked throat, and stricken with
 illness.
It is inappropriate to say the guru is ignorant.
If you do, for one minor eon it will be impossible
To meet with the path to enlightenment.
It is inappropriate to deceive the guru,
For you will be born in a land of mutes,
With your tongue cut out by a new sword.
To the guru, the vajra master,
Do not say anything untoward.
If you do, you will born between crushing mountains.
Do not break a well-spoken command.
If you do, you will be born in the realm of Incessant
 Torment.
If you abuse the guru with harsh words,
You will live for six thousand eons
In the horrible place of agonized screams.
If you do not abide by what the guru says,
You will experience karmic suffering for a long time.
The application of many exaggerations or denigrations
Is tantamount to killing one hundred ordained monks,
And your fall will be to the Hell of Incessant Torment alone.
Saying, "I am better than you,"

Will bring you to hell for extended eons.
Utter various dishonest insults
And you will constantly fall into the Hell of Cut Throats.
These, as well, are physical samaya vows.
To rectify impairments, write one hundred thousand dha-
    rani mantras,
Place them inside a stupa,
And hang many pairs of bells.

And:

Mentally observe the following pledges:
Covet your guru's possessions
And you will experience intolerable hunger and thirst
In the realm of spirits for two eons.
Compete with the guru and you will be born
In the impassable defile of samsara,
Even if you practice the Dharma diligently.
If you harbor animosity,
You will be born in the Hell of Slicing Swords.
If you think the vajra master has great desire and
    attachment,
You will wander throughout all the lower realms.
If you think the vajra master has great anger and hatred,
You will be boiled in the sixty hells.
If you think the vajra master is narrow-minded,
You will be born in the Wailing Hell.
If you think the vajra master's appetite is never sated,
You will be born in the Hell of Incessant Torment.
If you think the vajra master has great pride,
You will be born in a place of quarrels.
If you think the vajra master is ineloquent,
You will never find the unsurpassable path.
If you think of the vajra master in terms of four faults,[4]
The faults of your negative attitude will always be revealed.
You will be killed by malevolent gods and serpent beings

And swiftly fall to the hell realms.
These, as well, are the physical samayas.
To repair impairments, at the night's end,
Accumulate one hundred thousand written supplications
    and praises
And one hundred thousand written words of confession;
Continually maintain the yearly and monthly rites.

In a similar manner, even though your qualities of realization and transmission may enable you to do so, you should not directly work for the welfare of others until you have obtained the consent of your guru; you should merely include them in your aspirations. The same tantra continues:

Furthermore, the deeds of the vajra master
Are not to be engaged in by the student.
If the guru's disciples are taken as [one's own] students,
You will fall to hell, with no refuge.
The vajra master is the king of Dharma,
And a king's work is to maintain his dominion.
Similarly, the six roots of the Dharma are
The two roots of the lower vehicles—
Cultivating bodhichitta and imparting the vows,
The two roots of the superior vehicle—
The bestowal of empowerment and introduction,
And the two roots of the vehicles in common—
Consecration and the elevation of place.
These teachings are the dominion
That are to be maintained by the vajra master king.
Hence, if these six roots
Are enacted by a student
Within twelve leagues in the four directions,
He or she will be born beneath
The great Mount Meru for sixty-eight eons.
"Why?" you may ask. Because this is like a subject
Seizing power from a king;

The guru's qualities will be eclipsed by the student's.
In the future, he or she will have nowhere to go
Except hell, so I have taught.
If the vajra master's influence
Does not extend beyond twelve leagues,
You may be empowered a regent with consent.
Yet, you should meet in a year's time,
Offering pleasing enjoyments with faith.

This is also addressed in the *Condensed Meaning of the Tantras*:

Though your qualities may be inconceivable,
If the guru has not granted his or her consent,
Stay silent and abandon all activities
Of scholarship and accomplishment.
Though you may possess wealth and riches,
Abandon food and clothing, and with fortitude
Adopt a humble position and reject posturing,
And carry out what is said to the letter.

If your guru gives a command, you must carry it out, even if it is a taboo, negative behavior that appears inappropriate from a worldly point of view. The *Tantra of the Self-Occurring* states:

Theft, robbery, warfare, violence,
Beatings, insulting others, acting insane,
And shameless, immoral acts—
All manner of taboo activities—
If the command is given, you must do them.
Even if you are ordered to work for profit, take a wife,
Envy, quarrel, do manual labor,
Or tether calves and sheep,
Do what was said without hesitation.

Uneducated people, or those with preconceptions, may think that teaching in such a manner isn't befitting for a teacher, but this is not the case. You should look for a teacher who has the qualifications spelled out in the collected tantras. Do not make the mistake of choosing a teacher based purely on personal preference, or of following those with many afflictions simply because they are famous. As the *Complete Condensation of the Sadhanas* states:

> In future times,
> Beings with inferior merit
> Will not find an enlightened teacher.
> Instead, they will encounter
> An undisciplined, evil master.
> Avoid making this mistake.

So long as this is not the case, you can be sure that a guru with the full range of qualifications is an enlightened being, no matter how he or she may appear on the surface. Such a guru will not teach you to do something wrong. Even if this were to happen, the intention would certainly be to tame your mind. Hence, you should act without hesitation, just as the great scholar Naropa served the lotus feet of Tilopa.[5] Therefore, it makes perfect sense to carry out your teacher's commands. The same tantra states:

> Serve the guru, explain the Dharma,
> Impart the vows, maintain the monastery,
> Gather the retinue and students together,
> Benefit others, viewing happiness and suffering to be of
> one taste.
> Maintain and disseminate the Dharma for mountain
> retreat.
> It is said that you should be consistent
> Even in the case of sickness or death.
> Whatever you are ordered to do, carry it out.

Similarly, you should pay homage to the guru whether he or she is living or dead. A tantra states:

If the guru has passed on, make commemorative offerings.
If the guru is alive, make pleasing offerings.
Failing to make a commemorative offering once the guru
 has died
Is a major degeneration of the root samayas, and liberation
From the lower realms will be impossible.
If these degenerate, make 108 images
Of the guru's form, and make the three offerings
Uninterruptedly for six months:
The offering of body is one hundred thousand prostrations.
The offering of speech is one thousand confessions.
The offering of mind is one hundred butter lamps.
First, make these offerings for six months,
And then maintain the ceremony at the prescribed times.

And:

Diligently serve and venerate
The guru's spouse, children, and brothers and sisters
As equal, similar, and a third [as important as the guru],
 respectively.
If this degenerates, offer one hundred confessions.

With a mind made workable by the momentum of merit, bring
both attitude and conduct to bear on the various aspects of ethi-
cal discernment, examining them with great care. Through this, the
excellent qualities of the five paths will be in the palm of your hand.
Then, you will enjoy the temporary splendors of the higher realms
and will proceed unimpededly to the level of definite goodness.
Furthermore, when you dwell in the presence of such enlightened
gurus and offer them your full veneration with a great accumulation
of merit, studying and contemplating on a vast scale constitutes the
path of accumulation. By tasting the nectar of these teachings just as
they have been taught, you will instantly merge with nonconceptual
wisdom; this will bring you to the path of connection. The nature

of reality is nothing whatsoever. When this great definitive truth, which is difficult to grasp using metaphors, is revealed directly via the four symbolic methods and other means, you will reach the path of insight. Once you have conquered any obstacles and sidetracks involving falling into a dualistic extreme, such as meditating or not meditating on this nature, you will come to know an all-pervasive, self-occurring meditation in which there is no meeting or parting. This will bring you to the path of cultivation. Finally, you will reach the end of your training by bringing this realization to a point of culmination by means of the four great confidences; in taking hold of your own state, in which there is no meditation, you will arrive at the path beyond training. The tantras state:

> Dwelling in the presence of an enlightened guru
> And serving and respecting him or her completely
> Is what is meant by the term "path of accumulation."

> Merging the enlightened guru's explanation of the meaning
> And practical instructions with your being
> Is what I teach to be the "path of connection."

> Seeing the definitive truth in this life
> Through the four types of introduction
> Is what I explain to be the "path of insight."

> Meditation without something to meditate on
> And meditation in which there is something to meditate on—
> These two being beyond meeting and parting
> Is what I teach to be the "path of cultivation."

> The four great confidences, the realization of a buddha—
> Having perfected the way of nonabiding—
> Is what I explain to be the "path of culmination."

The state of complete omniscience comes only from an enlightened guru. Therefore, just like the bodhisattva Sadaprarudita, who served the noble Dharmodgata; like the great master Nagarjuna, who was liberated in a single session due to his great devotion to the Mahabrahmin Saraha; like Atisha, who underwent incalculable sufferings on the high seas just to request teachings on bodhichitta from his guru Serlingpa; like Naropa, who followed Tilopa, and the exalted Milarepa, who served Marpa, willingly do whatever your guru commands, enduring hardships just as they did and offering whatever you have to the guru.

If you have the wisdom to know how to regard whatever arises with devotion, you will see that the guru is an expert when it comes to the vital points of the instructions, that he or she has attained the warmth of meditative experience, possesses great blessings and power, and is highly realized. At this present time, in fact, the guru is Samantabhadra himself, and thus we are very fortunate. Without acting like a startled yak,[6] you should now serve your guru with the utmost respect. Over and over again, think to yourself, "I must do whatever it takes to receive the profound instructions and gain realization equal to my guru's!"

When this has taken birth in your being and the guru's blessings have infused your being, first the mind will turn away from samsara. Second, it will open up to the expanse of wisdom. Third, realization of the co-emergent will manifest, and you will understand all the conventional phenomena that can be known and be self-liberated from your bonds; fabricated assumptions about the awareness of absolute wisdom will be severed from within.

The approach of serving a guru described above is intended solely for novice practitioners. In the context of the main practice, the offering of practice is the only one of the three forms of pleasing the teacher with which you should concern yourself. On this point, the *Complete Condensation of the Eight Instructions* states:

> Now, to please the guru with a skillful,
> Specific, and extraordinary method
> Is to work toward the attainment of enlightenment.
> To carry out exactly what the guru commands,
> Offer your pledge to practice

For one, six, or twelve months,
Or one, six, or twelve years.
Similarly, render service to the guru
And work for the welfare of beings
In a way that is in harmony with the scriptures.
Safeguard and ensure the integrity of the three forms
Of the Buddha's teachings, thus it is said.
If you let go of mental resistance
To carrying out the command without hesitation,
Your goals will be attained without hindrance.

In this way, you should establish a framework by studying the teachings you have received, cut through to their very essence by contemplating, and take them to heart through meditation. One must venture forth to the state of a master siddha by coming to a definitive understanding via these three forms of knowledge. Nevertheless, novice practitioners who are unable to actually put this into practice should make it the goal of their aspirations. Those who are able to practice in the correct manner should do so in accordance with the place, time, and circumstances in which they find themselves. This approach is discussed in the *Flower Ornament Sutra*, in the Ancient Translation School's ocean-like collection of tantras, such as the *Complete Empowerment of Vajrapani Tantra* and the *Arrangement of the One Hundred Thousand Samaya Vows*, and in all the various uncompiled key instructions. All of these teach that casting aside that which should be practiced is the root of all problems and that taking up the practice is the source of all good things. Hence, this is held to be the root of the path.

Meditation

From the *Child Scripture*:

> If you obtain instructions but do not meditate, you will
> definitely not attain buddhahood. Hence, you should
> abandon laziness and meditate one-pointedly.

By serving your teacher as if he or she were as precious as your own
eyes, you may receive all kinds of profound and vast instructions.
However, if you fail to lay aside distractions and meditate on them
one-pointedly, a merely superficial, theoretical understanding will
not produce [a true understanding of] the meaning of that which
possesses the excellence of all aspects. The *Buddha Avatamsaka Sutra*
states:

> Just like an expert ferryman
> Who delivers many people,
> Yet who himself dies in that very place,
> Without meditation, such is the Dharma.

Likewise, the master Aryadeva explains:

> Those who crossed to the far shore
> Of study for millions of eons,
> When looking back on their blessings
> Will see that this does not lead to realization.

Similarly, even the Sage's own attendant Ananda did not progress beyond the level of stream-enterer to attain the level of a foe-destroyer until the time of the First Assembly,[1] despite the fact that he had served at the lotus feet of Shakyamuni himself and had crossed over a virtual ocean of teachings. According to the *Complete Empowerment of Vajrapani Tantra*, this noble being was in fact an emanation of Vajrapani. If that is so, then the assertion that ordinary, immature beings like us could attain enlightenment without meditating is pure rubbish!

Therefore, to awaken the profound wisdom that has been present in your mind from the very beginning, you need to be guided along the profound path of symbol, meaning, and sign by a fully qualified enlightened teacher, and after that, you must train without letting yourself get distracted. Think to yourself, "I won't fall prey to laziness and sloth for even a moment! I won't procrastinate, concerning myself with food, future plans, hopes, or fears! I won't let myself get lost in a state of apathy!" Properly restrain your mind with these thoughts, and like the focus of a mother searching for her lost only son, don't get sidetracked by the concerns of this life for even a moment; trample laziness underfoot! Devour procrastination and conquer sloth, and stay in isolated places like a wounded animal or a rhinoceros with the heartfelt thought "I must one-pointedly practice these instructions that I have heard!"

Negativity

From the *Child Scripture*:

> Ponder the fact that worldly wealth is like honey made
> with poison; the extent to which one enjoys it is the extent
> to which one engenders suffering.

The *Way of the Bodhisattva* states:

> Though we think we want to be rid of suffering,
> Suffering is exactly what we rush straight toward.
> And though we want to be happy, in our ignorance,
> We destroy our own happiness like an enemy.

We are completely ignorant when it comes to knowing right from
wrong. Though we want to be happy, what we do brings only suffering. An example of this is a moth that is attracted to the light of
a butter lamp but ends up dying, scorched in its flame; or a bee that
craves nectar and suckles a flower, only to become stuck or caught
and killed as the flower closes up; or a deer, killed while entranced
by the sound of flute; or a fish, drawn by the taste of the bait on the
tip of a fisherman's hook, dying on dry land; or an elephant that gets
stuck and dies on the muddy shores of a lake, having longed for the
cool sensation of its waters. The *Treasury of Dohas* states:

> See them to be like a fish or a moth,
> An elephant, bee, or deer.

Thus, the afflictions lie dormant, hidden in our mind-streams like salt dissolved in water. Someone with a chronic illness may appear to be fine when the illness is in remission, but when he or she eats something or encounters some circumstance that reactivates it, the illness will manifest once again. In a similar manner, our attachment and fixation toward the five desirable sense objects creates a karmic link with the three lower realms, prompting us to engage solely in the negative actions that will cause us to be reborn there. It is only fitting, then, that we will eventually have to experience the suffering that results from this nonvirtue, despite our wishes to the contrary.

To rid ourselves of this suffering, we need to abandon negativity once and for all, for it is this negativity that is the cause and source of suffering. Nevertheless, taking medicine to alleviate symptomatic pain will not suffice to cure a disease; the illness's causes, conditions, essence, temperature, and so on, must be precisely identified. Only then may a medical treatment be properly administered. Just so, what we need to recognize here is the negative act, or nonvirtue, that precipitates our suffering. The *Treasury of Higher Dharma* explains further:

> Virtue and nonvirtue, in all their forms,
> The path of karma is taught to be tenfold.

Nonvirtue can be summarized under ten categories: the three physical nonvirtues are (1) taking life, (2) stealing, and (3) sexual misconduct; the four verbal nonvirtues are (4) lying, (5) divisive speech, (6) harsh words, and (7) idle chatter; and the three mental nonvirtues are (8) covetousness, (9) malice, and (10) wrong views.

1. TAKING LIFE

Generally speaking, it goes without saying that killing any sentient being, regardless of the species, constitutes the nonvirtue of taking life. The taking of life is subdivided into three categories: the intent to kill, the act of killing, and the culmination of the act. If all three of these are present, all forms of the nonvirtue of taking life are complete, and the karmic ripening will be extremely weighty. The *intent to kill* is the occurrence of a murderous desire. The *act of killing* may involve a deluded mind-set yet no murderous intent, such as when you step on a being and it dies. Hence, the number of sentient beings that we have killed is beyond reckoning.

Furthermore, it won't suffice to experience a single result of this nonvirtue, as each act has a fully ripened result, a result that resembles its cause, and a dominant result. As exemplified by the five acts of immediate retribution, such as killing one's mother, father, vajra master, or a foe-destroyer, the fully ripened result of taking life will be a rebirth in one of the three lower realms, depending upon the intensity of the act. As the result that resembles its cause, even if one manages to attain a pleasurable existence, one will have a short life. As the dominant result, the food, drink, and medicine one ingests will have no potency.

2. Stealing

The basis for stealing is a valuable item, such as gold, that you do not own and is in the possession of another. Such objects may be taken by force, deceit, or stealth. The first occurs when someone is violently robbed or when something is taken as punishment. The second refers to extracting a hefty interest when doing business or to miscalculating in your own favor. Taking by stealth refers to either outright theft or various deceitful means such as saying, "I really need that thing you have, but I don't have one," in order to acquire the desired item, ultimately resulting in the notion that you have achieved your aims. The fully ripened result of stealing is the same as stated in the previous section. The result that resembles its cause is that one will be bereft of wealth. The dominant result is that one's crops and fruit will dwindle.

3. Sexual Misconduct

Sexual misconduct includes relations with someone who is upholding a vow [of celibacy], someone who is in a committed relationship with someone else, or a relative. In this day and age, it can be difficult to determine who one's relatives are, so the Vinaya stipulates that anyone to whom you are related up to seven generations back is a relative. Beyond that, they are not relatives. Thus, sexual relations with relatives up to seven generations back are to be abandoned. Furthermore, although your sexual partner may be your wife or some other legitimate partner, having intercourse in front of a religious object, in the mouth, or anus, and so forth, are not permitted, nor is having intercourse at an inappropriate time, such as during pregnancy or while holding the one-day precepts.

With sexual misconduct, one first conceives of such an act and then, prompted by an emotional affliction, one applies oneself to the execution of the unchaste act that one desires. The act is complete when the genitals unite. The fully ripened result of sexual misconduct is a rebirth in one of the three lower realms. The result that resembles its cause is that one will have a promiscuous spouse. As the dominant result, one will be born in filthy swamps and terrifying places.

4. LYING

Lying includes lies that create downfalls and excessive lies, such as pretending that one has enlightened qualities when one does not, that one has attained accomplishment when one has not, or that one understands the Dharma when one does not. These are exemplified by the lies of fake gurus, who may state that they have seen deities when they have not, that they have attained levels of realization though they have not, or that they have supernatural powers that they do not possess.

Here, one first forms the desire to tell a tale, motivated by one of the afflictions. The execution is to show some expression, through either gesture or speech, and the act is complete when the other person understands the meaning [that was communicated]. The fully ripened result of lying is a rebirth in one of the three lower realms. The result that resembles its cause is to be the subject of gossip. As the dominant result, one will be born in places that are frightenting and full of deception.

5. Divisive Speech

Just like the tale told in the sutras, where a fox sows discord between a bull and an ox that are friends, causing them to dislike one another, divisive speech starts out with the firm resolve of one of the afflictions, and the subsequent desire to divide those who are close or intimate, or those who have neutral relations. The execution is to say something that is capable of creating a division, or to create discord surreptitiously using mantras or substances that instigate disputes. The act is complete when the other person understands the meaning [that was communicated]. Its fully ripened result is rebirth in one of the three lower realms. The result that resembles its cause is to have few loved ones. The dominant result is that one will inhabit uneven places that are difficult to traverse.

6. Harsh Words

An example of a precursor for harsh words is the sight of an unattractive person or someone of low stature. Motivated by one of the three afflictions, one gets the urge to proclaim the person's faults openly, and then puts this into action by saying something harsh. The act is complete when one's insult strikes his or her heart like an arrow and its meaning has been understood. Its fully ripened result is the same as with the aforementioned nonvirtues. The result that resembles its cause is that one will hear many insults. As the dominant result, one will live in a place with tree stumps, thorns, and other unpleasant things.

7. Idle Chatter

Idle chatter involves any topic of trifling importance, not including the three verbal nonvirtues mentioned above. After one conceives of such a topic, one of the afflictions brings about an irresistible urge to speak. The execution of this act may be to recite the evil mantras of the Brahmins or the Jain treatises, or to frivolously talk about war, banditry, and other irrelevant and distracting subjects. This also includes singing songs or putting on plays motivated by desire, or a practitioner flattering another in order to acquire goods. The act is complete once the meaning is understood. The fully ripened result of idle chatter is a rebirth in one of the three lower realms. The result that resembles its cause is that one's words will lack strength. The dominant result is that fruit trees bear no fruit.

8. COVETOUSNESS

Covetousness starts with the perception of another's wealth, which causes one to experience a desirous and spiteful mind-set. One hoards and clings dearly to one's own wealth. The overwhelming urge brought on by a fivefold affliction overpowers any sense of shame or wrong, and one greedily and obsessively thinks, "If only I had that person's wealth!" The ensuing aspiration completes the act. The fully ripened result of covetousness is the same as was previously mentioned. The result that resembles its cause is that one's hopes will not be fulfilled. As the dominant result, one's prosperity will gradually diminish.

9. MALICE

The objective basis of malice is an individual whom one perceives as unpleasant. In essence, malice is a mind-set of intense, enduring hatred; a vindictive mind-set that continually obsesses [about its object] in a distorted manner; a prideful mind-set that cannot tolerate harmful persons; an aggressive mind-set that thinks, "How wonderful it would be to kill him or beat her!"; and a mind-set that overpowers any sense of shame or wrong.

Motivated by one of these fivefold afflictions, one applies oneself to the execution of the act, which may involve capturing, imprisoning, or murdering the individual, and so on. The act is complete when one decides to carry out the act when one is actually able to do so. The fully ripened result of malice is a birth in one of the three lower realms. The result that resembles its cause is intense terror. As the dominant result, one will be attacked many times by both human and nonhuman forces.

10. WRONG VIEWS

The objective basis of wrong views is infallible doctrines such as the law of karmic causality. With assertions like those made by the Nihilists, one perceives such doctrines as false and desires to deprecate them, motivated by one of the afflictions. The execution comes when one believes these doctrines to be utterly false, thereby confirming one's suspicions. The act is complete when one feels conviction about this. The fully ripened result of wrong views is a rebirth in whichever of the lower realms is most fitting. The result that resembles its cause is ignorance of the genuine view. As the dominant result, good and evil will be mistaken.

Similarly, when the ten nonvirtuous acts are classified in terms of their respective level of severity, all of the following are extremely severe: motivated by an intensely afflicted mind-set, to murder extraordinary persons such as one's guru (which is serious from a spiritual point of view) or one's parents (which is serious from a worldly point of view); or to deceive, steal from, and create divisions between such persons; to insult them; or to harbor a covetous or malicious attitude toward them. Likewise, to have sexual relations with someone holding the vows of discipline or any other unacceptable partner; to lie and sow discord in order to create a schism within the sangha, as Devadatta did; to assert that there is no such thing as a foe-destroyer; to kill a large animal motivated by a desire for its flesh and blood; to steal many things and those that are very valuable; and to delight in negativity without confessing and committing [to refrain from such acts in the future]. Such acts are extremely weighty, and the opposites of these acts are light.

By way of explanation, the bodhisattva Padma writes:

> The ten nonvirtues and the five acts of immediate
>   retribution,
> The five close and four weighty acts,
> The eight mistaken acts and severe misdeeds—
> Even at the cost of your life, abandon even the most minor
>   of these.

> The vows that are in harmony with the ten virtues,
> Those of the layman, novice, one-day retreatant, fully
> ordained monk,
> And others of individual liberation, also bodhisattva vows
> and those of Secret Mantra—
> Embrace and safeguard the vows you have taken. If you
> desire liberation,
> Safeguard them carefully, as you would your own life.

With a thorough understanding of the classifications just discussed, which pertain to acts and their respective results, examine your mind to clearly identify which of them is the most dominant.

Meditate until your interest and enthusiasm prompts you to think, "Alas! I've amassed an immeasurable amount of such negativity up until now, but since my acts have not been embraced with mindful awareness, I've wandered in a state of indifference. Like a barbarian, I never knew that I was accumulating karma; what a huge mistake! As represented by the ten nonvirtues, from here on out, whenever a negative mind-set occurs, whether subtle or coarse, I will apply an antidote and turn the other way. Yet this alone will not suffice; I will also work courageously to practice the opposite of such negativity— virtue! I will arouse diligence so intense that it is as though my hair or clothes are on fire, and I will apply myself to the ten virtuous actions, such as renouncing killing."

The master Vasubandhu once wrote:

> Because observable phenomena and so forth
> Will be experienced, there are three definite types.

There are stories of evil people like Devadatta, Shasarakisha, Shri-dhara, and others [who committed such extremely negative acts] that they had conscious experiences of going to hell without leaving their bodies behind. Such evil people have created karma that is sure to bring them a rebirth in the lower realms.

Unless you are such a person, you should think, "Alas, to attain liberation and omniscience one needs to completely do away with the very roots of such nonvirtue, but if I think about it, in this lifetime alone I have consciously amassed so much negativity. And this doesn't reflect even a fraction of what I've accumulated in my previous lives! It's only logical that I've amassed an inconceivable amount of negativity for the sake of my friends, students, subjects, community, and so on. What's more, the results of these acts will be experienced by me alone; these acts that I've consciously committed cannot be shared with anyone else." On this point, Master Nagarjuna explains:

> Do not commit negative actions for Brahmins, monks,
>   gods,
> Guests, your parents, queens, or companions—
> For there will be no one with whom to share the result
> When it ripens as a rebirth in hell.

That being so, you may think to yourself, "Oh no, not me! Not me! It looks like once I pass away, I'll have no choice but to endure the lower realms!" Inevitably, you will sink into despair, and it is at this moment that you will realize the implicit harm of karmic consequences.

Nowadays people merely pay lip service to virtue and nonvirtue without directly recognizing the most basic principles concerning what they should do and not do. In this sense, they are hardly better than barbarians. In truth, this is nothing more than a state of apathy. Due to the kindness of our enlightened teachers, however, we now see that our actions and their results do not just disappear. How fortunate!

It isn't enough, however, simply to see that and become fearful and withdrawn. With the four powers complete, you need to confess earnestly and restrain yourself, with a firm sense of regret for what you have done. You should then devote yourself to enlightened activities. Our Teacher, with his great compassion and skillful methods, said that if you do not err in terms of what to do and not do, past negativity can be purified through earnest confession and self-restraint, even if one has engaged in extremely violent acts in the past, such as those with immediate retribution. *Letter to a Friend* states:

One without conscience in the past
Who later on becomes conscientious
Is a thing of beauty, like the moon revealed by parting
    clouds,
As was Nanda, Angulimala, Darshaka, and Udayana.

The Buddha's relative Nanda was extremely attached to his wife, Pundarika. To address the situation, the Thus-Gone skillfully led him both to a divine city and to hell. This tamed Nanda's desire, and he eventually became a foe-destroyer. Angulimala killed 999 people, and Ajatashatru killed his father, Bimbisara. Though they had committed acts of immediate retribution, they were purified through confession and restraint and both later attained the level of foe-destroyers. Udayana killed his own mother, but from that moment on, he regretted what he had done and began to behave in a morally correct manner. He ended up being born in hell for as long as it takes to throw a silk ball; he later attained the level of a stream-enterer.

Accordingly, as soon as you recall such negative actions, you should cultivate a deep sense of regret and exert yourself in the methods of confession. This is a most profound point, so you should train in the recitation of the *Sutra in Three Parts*.

Furthermore, in the context of these instructions, failure to recognize the aforementioned ten nonvirtues and their corresponding results must be avoided. Whenever these come to mind, the antidote is to recite the *Sutra in Three Parts* while adhering to the vital points of the four powers. Alternate meditating on these two practices over and over again. From now on, be mindful and aware of all nonvirtue, and crush any negative thoughts as soon as they arise. In the context of the main practice, always follow the example set by Atisha Dipamkara: confess in the morning the negativity that you accumulate in the morning, and confess at bedtime the negativity that you accumulate in the afternoon. Don't let negativity or downfalls stay with you for even a day!

Some people take this to mean that simply confessing in this manner is enough. With this understanding, they behave wantonly, with no sense of restraint when it comes to immoral behavior and nonvirtue. However, it is a grave mistake to think that merely reciting a few words of confession morning and night will suffice, for doing so will overwhelm the confession outlined above, in which one confesses with a remorseful attitude using the four powers. It will also result in the instant degeneration of the mind-set of restraint, where one thinks: "I won't do this again even if it costs me my life!" Hence, this is a misguided belief that eclipses all the infallible doctrines concerning the interdependence of actions and their results.

The terms and principles that have been presented thus far should be given serious consideration. If all worldly activities fail to repulse you, like food repulses someone with jaundice, what you have heard are just quotations and what you have read are just words. This will not allow your mind to reach the level of mastery. The Great Master of Oddiyana said:

> Seek out whatever Buddhist transmissions and teachings
> there are.
> When you study the sacred Dharma, if you don't use the
> right attitude
> To grasp the terms and principles, it will be like pouring
> water
> Onto an upside-down vessel: none will go inside.
> When the anguish of samsara wells up, they won't be of any
> benefit!

However wonderful worldly wealth may be, like a candle in the wind, a dew drop in summer, a flash of lightning in the sky, or last night's dream, it is utterly impermanent and unreal. Hence, you should always stay in isolated places and cultivate a sense of disenchantment, trusting with all your heart that whatever you have will be enough. Take refuge in the fact that you will be joyful when sick and happy when dying. Let people say what they will, as if they are talking about a corpse. Like a wandering leper, yearn to be totally on your own, without even song birds to keep you company. Occupy your mind with meditating on your enlightened guru's instructions. The Great Master of Oddiyana said:

This world is a land of sadness;
The wonderful joy and happiness of beings,
Like a dew drop in summer or wealth in a dream,
Is unreal and swiftly gone.
From such things come distorted desires and carelessness.
So always cultivate a disenchanted frame of mind.
Those who hold worldly splendor in great esteem
Are of a class with inferior merit.
Your heart, like a rotten tree,
Will never bear the fruit of liberation.
Alas, how sad! The mind that thinks of the wealth
And prosperity of this life as wonderful and lasting,
The mind that thinks it to be stable and excellent,
Belongs to the most base of all immature beings!
Who in this world could be more foolish than that?
No one in the past and no one in the future!

Wisdom

The *Child Scripture* states:

> "In this way, I will abandon outer and inner distractions
> and settle into a nonconceptual absorption. As my expe-
> rience evolves, this will last longer and longer. Through
> this, I will never separate from this very point!" With this
> thought, cultivate a sense of certainty and train the mind
> in this seventh point.

And from the conclusion:

> Using nonconceptuality to train the mind is the unsur-
> passable gateway to the path of concentration.

The *Sphere of Liberation* states:

> Drawing in the upper energy brings mastery over
>   appearance.
> Drawing in the lower energy brings mastery over
>   emptiness.
> Retaining and stirring the central energy brings an
>   integrated unity.

By leaving appearances on the outside and awareness on the inside,
with karmic energies acting as the mind's steed in between, sentient

beings wander in a state of dualistic fixation. In their delusion, they experience the continuous chain of samsara. Using the swift and profound path of the Vajra Vehicle, one can learn to control the movements of the karmic energies. These key instructions allow one to recognize innate wisdom in a very direct, powerful way; one need not rely on the inferential concentrations of the lower vehicles, where one must apply reasoning to the web of conceptuality for an extended period of time.

These key instructions contain three parts:

- ► Accessing the nonconceptuality of bliss-emptiness
- ► Accessing the nonconceptuality of clarity-emptiness
- ► Accessing the nonconceptuality of reality itself

THE NONCONCEPTUALITY OF BLISS-EMPTINESS

For the first, seat yourself in the seven-point meditation posture and visualize the central channel running straight up and down the interior of your body, which should be clear and empty like the interior of an inflated balloon. This channel has four qualities: it is as straight as the trunk of a plantain tree, as delicate as the petal of a lotus, as blue as a cloudless sky, and as radiant as the flame of an oil lamp.

As you meditate on this channel, visualize a white HAM syllable at its opening on the crown of your head. At its lower opening below your navel, visualize a red AH syllable. While practicing the four applications, press the upper energy down and draw the lower energy up. Imagine that this causes fire to blaze forth from the AH syllable at your navel, causing the HAM syllable at the upper opening to melt. This, in turn, produces a steady flow of nectar that streams down and permeates the four chakras and all the minor channels, triggering the wisdom of bliss-emptiness. Finally, fix your mind on a white AH syllable at your heart center, cut the thread of discursive thought, and rest one-pointedly. This will produce the wisdom of emptiness, the knowledge that utilizes the skillful means of bliss. Until you have familiarized yourself with this state, train in short, frequent sessions.

The Nonconceptuality of Clarity-Emptiness

To train the mind in nonconceptual clarity-emptiness, you first need to draw out the poisonous elemental energies by expelling the stale breath three or nine times. Next, as you inhale, imagine that all solid external appearances melt into shimmering light and merge into clear blue space, which then fills your entire body. Finally, press the upper energies firmly down, draw the lower energy slightly upward, and join the two together. This meditation will generate an experience of clarity-emptiness.

According to the Glorious One from Samye [Longchenpa], a vital point of this practice is to meditate that the energies are hot if a cold sensation is dominant, and cool if a hot sensation is more intense.

Those who are fond of more elaborate forms of practice may wish to meditate on the energies of each individual element, as outlined in the *Child Scripture: The Lamp That Clarifies Wisdom*. However, the *Essential Commentary on Mind Training* from the Guru's Quintessence explains:

> The energy of space, however, is good to practice at all times, and as physical sensations are included in these two (hot and cold), this is sufficient for practice.

This form of vase breathing is the source of all good qualities. The *Jewel Rosary of Advice* states:

> Since the central channel is supreme, these perceptible experiences are not revealed. Yet, again, without exhaling, inhale and hold the breath. This will cause the energies to pass through the right and left channels into the lower aperture of the central channel, which looks like the lower half of the Tibetan letter ཆ. As the energies enter the path of the central channel, the unmistaken realization of the first ground will arise. Each of the three signs of entering, abiding, and dissolving will manifest. When the first knot

of the central channel dissolves and the energies enter, the qualities of the first level will manifest. When the mind-energies abide there, the qualities of the second level will arise. Once the mind-energies completely dissolve there, dualistic thought patterns will be purified like space and all of the qualities of wisdom will unfold.

In the short term, penetrating the vital points of the vase breath will result in a long life, few illnesses, a body that is healthy and as swift as a bird, and other such qualities. All the qualities of the energies must be elicited through utilizing the vase breath, so, Tsogyal, you must pierce the vital point of all energetic meditations and the vase breath!

THE NONCONCEPTUALITY OF REALITY ITSELF

To train the mind in the nonconceptuality of reality itself, relax the body and mind from deep within and keep your gaze fixed. This will allow you to remain in a state free from all the comings and goings of thought activity. Without making any deliberate effort to restrain the breath, fill the navel area with central energy. This is an extremely profound key instruction. The *Jewel Rosary of Advice* states:

Listen, Tsogyal, with your body in a cross-legged posture, slightly inhale the lower energy, press the upper energy slightly down, and fill the navel area with the central energy. The merit of this energetic practice is that wisdom will remain in its natural state.

You can use this practice as an aid to whatever meditation you do, whether you are meditating on your body in the development stage, on your mind as luminosity, or any other practice. This energetic meditation automatically accomplishes the controlling, guiding, and distributing of the energetic essences. Dualistic thought patterns will automatically be purified, and awareness will be freed from the three faults of torpor, dullness, and agitation. Cataracts and other problems with the sense faculties will not occur, illnesses related to phlegm and bile will not strike, and a bloated or upset stomach will clear up automatically. Epidemics and other contagious diseases will be eliminated, as will lice infestations. Through this energetic meditation, your life span will last as long as the sun and moon.

Thus, visualize your body as the yidam deity. Without leaning to one side or slouching, press the energy down and inflate the navel area. Stare into space, and rest your consciousness in a state of original purity. This is referred to as "the energetic practice of great wisdom" and "the energetic practice of distinguishing awareness from mind." When practicing these energetic meditations, pull your sides slightly inward and keep your navel area filled. You should also maintain this "fullness" whenever you inhale, fill, or practice any other energetic activity. By penetrating the vital point here with one-pointed concentration, the upper and lower energies will naturally be led into [the central channel].

Keeping the navel filled throughout will also function as a support for mindfulness. You should even maintain this fullness when you meditate on a yidam deity. When you recite essence mantras, do so while maintaining this fullness. You should do this even when you meditate on the nonconceptual wisdom of reality itself. As you go about your day, walk around, lie down, sit, or do anything else, do not depart from this secret great wisdom.

As this passage shows, not only is the central energy relevant in the context of training the mind, it is also a wonderfully supportive factor for each and every step along the path to enlightenment. This is a very important point to remember.

Once you have trained your mind in these three forms of nonconceptuality, consciousness will stay fixed wherever it is directed, and you will be able to rest for longer and longer periods in a nonconceptual state like space. The extent to which this occurs will be the measure of your proficiency.

Conclusion

Do not allow these seven forms of training the mind to turn into mere platitudes or words left on the pages of a book. Bringing to mind a sense of disenchantment, remind yourself that the nature of samsara is as miserable as being thrown into a dungeon. Generally speaking, you should practice these seven at all times and places. More specifically, when you receive the maturing instructions or other such teachings, you should practice them for twenty-one, fourteen, or seven days at the very least. If you do not mingle the teachings with your mind, simply hearing the text read to you will not make your mind any more pliable. The Great Master of Oddiyana taught:

> This isn't just a matter of words. You have to practice letting samsara's transitory, impermanent, and painful nature permeate your mind, mingling it with your own disenchantment and renunciation. If you don't, it will be just as though you are plagued by hunger and thirst yet do not partake of the food and drink you have in your hands. Simply knowing that the food and drink will help you won't do a thing. It's clear that you need to actually eat and drink! Just so, by taking what you have understood to heart, you will understand that samsara is like being thrown into a dungeon and your mind will shift from temporary pleasures to long-lasting contentment alone.

As alluded to here, these stages will make the mind of the student completely disciplined and pliable. When this occurs, the door is opened to refuge and the rest of the unique preliminary practices, and to the special preliminaries [of the Heart Essence teachings], such as the separation of samsara [and nirvana].

As the path of the main practice, the latent potential of the four vajras that abides within the basic nature of beings is awakened via the interdependent ritual of symbols and methods: the empowerment that matures the student's mind-stream into infinite purity. The liberating instructions effortlessly link [the student's mind-stream] with the wisdom mind of the dharmakaya. All dualistic phenomena are introduced as the dynamic play of mindful awareness, free from arising, abiding, and cessation. The development stage of unified appearance-emptiness utilizes symbol, meaning, and sign to manifest ordinary appearances, sounds, and adventitious habitual tendencies as the manifold display of the three mandalas. The vital points and meaning of the tantras, scriptures, and key instructions are encapsulated in vajra words and must be taught explicitly via the six limits and the four modes. Using the pristine flow of teachings found in the four rivers of our own tradition, the Secret Mantra of the Ancient Translation School, one must skillfully utilize the methods that will transform the student's mind-stream into the nature of the three vajras.

At that time, a superior student will reach the full expression of the wisdom mind, having driven home the nail of unchanging self-awareness. Tolerating weariness, fatigue, and ingratitude, he or she will be empowered as a regent who carries out enlightened activities for the benefit of others, and will be conferred the authority of a vajra king.

Those of moderate [capacity] will not perfect their ability [to realize] the unity of appearance and awareness. Like a small stream in springtime, they will fluctuate between delusion and liberation, falling prey to various obstacles and false attainments, such as the demon of revelation, and other temporary circumstances. Without accomplishing their own benefit, they will make a show of benefiting others, engaging in a whole host of degenerate activities. Such people are guides on the path to hell, linking whomever they encounter with the lower realms. On the other hand, if they don't wander about in this manner but instead plant the victory banner of practice, they will be given the transmission that simultaneously accomplishes the two benefits.

THE STEPS TO LIBERATION — 99

At the very least, one must avoid falling into the habit of harboring a negative attitude and setting a bad example for the teachings, either in a general sense or specifically by doing negative things, such as behaving inappropriately for the sake of friends and food. Without becoming a heap of shortcomings, impervious to the Dharma and with broken [vows], one's conduct should be peaceful, subdued, and in harmony with the Dharma; the way one carries oneself should be an inspiration to others. One should also be able to distill the main principles of practice. In brief, one must be skilled in the methods and interdependent conditions involved in working with students and be able to outline the various stages of the clearly enumerated proscriptions and prohibitions that pertain to the samayas and vows, from those of individual liberation up to the Vajrayana. In ways such as these, one should bravely uphold the lineage of the Victorious One and be a worthy example of the conduct of a vajra holder, as were the great scholar Vimalamitra; the second buddha from Oddiyana, Padmasambhava; the omniscient king of Dharma Longchenpa; Ngari Mahapandita; and others.

Though they may trace their origins back to influential masters and others of good repute, those who are ignorant of such methods will themselves get caught up in afflictions, ignorance, and mistaken paths, and lead those with inferior merit to a similar fate. For this reason, I humbly request you well-known vajra masters of awareness and whatever hidden masters are out there to be aware of this manner of correctly elucidating the intent of the ocean of tantric principles and, with this awareness, to shoulder the victory banner of the teachings of the Ancient Translation School's Secret Mantra tradition. As stated in the Great Perfection tantras:

> In particular, train in all the practices
> And Dharma activities of this vehicle.
> Skillfully and with ease make them abandon
> All connections and attachments to samsaric activities.
> Bestow the elaborate and other empowerments,
> And have them approach and accomplish the yidam deities.
> Bestow the empowerments of the vehicles sequentially,

And have them distinguish body and speech
In rocky mountains or isolated charnel grounds.
Have them clear up uncertainties about their studies.
Bestow the unelaborate and other empowerments,
And train in time-appropriate conduct.
Grant precepts according to scripture.
Just as a mother
Nourishes her tiny infant,
With intense love and affection,
Offer the nectar-like milk of samaya.
Each and every teaching, without exception,
Radiates from a single point, a single root;
This one thing is the root of compassion.
Bestow the knowledge-wisdom empowerment.
Grant awareness in accord with aptitude.
Teach the bear-like activity.
To satisfy the mind of the student,
One should teach explicitly and elicit all signs.
Bestow the word and expression empowerments,
And casting off all activities with elaborations,
Relax and let go into nonelaboration.
Teach the deer-like activity.
Point out the heart of the definitive meaning
And strike the nail of unchanging self-awareness.
Empower [your disciples] as regents
And command them to benefit beings.
While resting in concentration oneself,
Train in all the disciplines of the bodhisattva,
In order to be of service to others.
At first, a student will not know
The divisions of the samaya vows,
Or the extent to which they are to be observed.
The guru should observe two-thirds of the samaya vows.
With only a rough knowledge, one-third,
And with a detailed knowledge, two-thirds

Are what the students themselves should observe.
At the right time, place, and circumstance,
The guru should explain to the student
All the various proscriptions and prohibitions.
The excellent qualities of this are inconceivable:
The lineage of all the buddhas will not be broken.
All the buddhas of the three times
Gradually arose by training in this manner.
Once a student has become your representative,
He or she will dredge samsara from its very depths.
The hook that leads all beings of the three realms,
Without exception, comes from this.
Therefore, may the interdependent connection
Between guru and student not go wrong!

Relying upon these practical methods as a ship to liberation—
the key instructions that liberate through explanation—the young
sea captain of my own mental discernment has spurned weariness
and fatigue, shouldered an altruistic mind-set, and ventured forth to
the supreme treasure isle of omniscience. May the victors and their
offspring be overjoyed from the expanse and grant me the jewel of
accomplishing the twofold benefit!

Amazing!
These precious freedoms and endowments are rare as
  a daytime star;
Even when found, like a candle flame in the wind,
They could vanish in an instant!
Pondering this, most people seem like mad sea captains.

The root of practice is renunciation.
So if you don't use the key points of mind training
To till the soil of your mind, hardened toward liberation,
When death comes and you beat your chest with regret,
  it will be too late!

When the karmic energies transform into the nature of
wisdom,
In tandem with the extinction of the dualistic perception
of samsara and nirvana,
The royal throne of dharmakaya is seized; for such a master
of awareness,
There is no need to train the mind with webs of concepts.

Yet, for those sieve-like vessels and the sounds of the flute
player—
That crooked class that believes the philosophies of the
Nihilists
And the immature beings who see happiness in samsara—
What else can one feel other than overwhelming love?

These instructions are not the explanations of a sophist,
words that seduce
The minds of the ignorant, like the water in a mirage that
fools an elephant.
They are instructions that allow us to cross over the ocean
of scriptures
And their meanings using the new ship of blessings of the
true tantra.

The learned and accomplished masters of times past are
gone, like the moon fading into the expanse,
And the teaching and accomplishment of scripture and
realization have set like the sun in the west.
The planets and stars now shine, competing for wealth and
power,
While the teachings of the Victorious One lie exhausted in
pitch darkness.

This song of the Chariots and the Seven Great Treasuries,
Intoxicated as they are with the sanctified liquor of the
nine vehicles,

This special wealth of the scripture and realization of the
    Omniscient One,
Who held the life force of the ancient translations, is now
    held by me.[1]

Therefore, if you wonder what this close lineage is,
Trime Özer[2] sits upon the crown of my head!
There is nothing between [me and] the lord of the
    teachings
Of the old translations in general and the Heart Essence in
    particular.

"This primordial protector, posing as a human,
Will clarify the essence of the teachings in this land."
Thus was it prophesied by the Lake-Born Vajra,[3]
In harmony with the sole intent of all masters of awareness.

First, fearing samsara, I turned my mind to liberation.
Then, I proceeded along the treacherous path of the infal-
    lible law of karma.
In the end, I gained realization, knowing the three spheres
    to be unreal.
This is the universal life story of siddhas.

From the five Precious Letters of the Heart Essence,
The intent of the Copper Letters is this seven-point mind
    training.
Whatever merit comes from explaining this topic on a vast
    scale,
I dedicate as a cause for attaining the jewel of omniscience!

The pristine (Trime) lotus grove of my mind inspired
    by the sun's rays (Özer),
I set forth this delightful grove as a gateway to the
    common path.

May this beautifully arranged, vastly spacious place of rest
  endure for a long time,
Bringing joy to its aspiring visitors!

———————

This text, *The Steps to Liberation*, carries the intent of the Precious
Copper Letters. It is both a general instruction manual on the
Great Perfection and a set of essential instructions on the seven
forms of training the mind that provide access to the common
preliminaries. Once, as I was applying myself diligently to the
essential practice at a sacred spot called Self-Arisen Lotus, I met
the wisdom form of the omniscient Trime Özer for the second
of what was to be three meetings. He gave me a volume of scripture and said, "This clarifies all that is hidden within the *Great
Chariot*"[4] and blessed me with the secret treasury of the fivefold
expanse. Based on this, I compiled a book of notes that I kept
secret for several years. Eventually, the Mad Vidyavira of Kongpo,
who was protected by descendants of Lord Nyang Nyima Özer's
lineage,[5] and one with pure perception named Wakindra provided
the auspicious circumstances [for the composition of this text]
with their fervent requests. Thus, 2,637 [years after] the second
buddha, the Great Master [Padmasambhava], was released from
the center of a lotus bud in the Sindhu Ocean, in the Male Wood-
Monkey Year, known as Tarana; 2,613 [years after] the awareness
holder Vajradharma, in Kilaka, the Earth-Monkey Year, turned the
wheel of Dharma of the oceanic secret tantras for the five noble
ones of the enlightened family—a god, a naga, a yaksha, a human
awareness holder, [and an ogre]—on the peak of Mount Malaya,
the king of mountains, and a rain of tantric texts fell on the roof
of the palace of Indrabhuti, the king of Sahor; 2,296 [years after]
the coming of the emanational display Garab Dorje, an emanated
reflection of the Invincible Protector, who was given the empowerment of direct anointment as the holder of all the tantric, textual, and instructional teachings by the heroic Lord of Secrets in

Krodha, the [female] Wood-Ox Year; 1,741 [years after] Vikrama, the Iron-Dragon Year that marked the birth of Vimalamitra, the crown ornament of five hundred great scholars who attained the rainbow body; and 453 years after the birth in Kilaka, the Earth-Monkey Year, of Longsal Trime of Glorious Samye, also known as the Omniscient Lord of Speech Longchenpa, who attained omniscience of the definitive meaning, in the Female Iron-Snake Year of the thirteenth sexagenary cycle, when the sun was abiding in the house of Scorpio, this text was completed by the renunciate yogi Dharma Lord Khyentse Özer (aka Rigdzin Jigme Lingpa) in the peaceful, naturally arisen stone abode of Tregu Cave at Samye Chimpu, the solitary place of [Padmasambhava's] speech. May it be virtuous from beginning to end!

Abbreviations

BT	*The Treasury of Knowledge: Book Six, Part Four: Systems of Buddhist Tantra*. Jamgön Kongtrul.
DK	sDe dge bka' 'gyur.
DMW	*Deity, Mantra, and Wisdom: Development Stage Meditation in Tibetan Buddhist Tantra*. Jigme Lingpa, Patrul Rinpoche, and Getse Mahapandita.
DR	*rDzogs rim chos drug bsdus don*. dPal sprul O rgyan 'jigs med chos kyi dbang po.
DT	sDe dge bstan 'gyur.
DZ	*The Practice of Dzogchen*. Longchen Rabjam.
EM	"The Ripening Empowerments." Tsele Natsok Rangdröl.
GP2	*Great Perfection*. Vol. 2, *Separation and Breakthrough*. Third Dzogchen Rinpoche.
HE	*Zab mo snying thig gi gnad thams cad bsdus pa'i don khrid lag len gsal ba*. bKra shis rgya mtsho.
JL	*bsKyed rim lha'i khrid kyi rnam par bzhag pa 'og min bgrod pa'i them skas*. 'Jigs med gling pa.
KG	*dPal sgrub pa chen po bka' brgyad kyi spyi don rnam par bshad pa dngos grub snying po*. 'Ju mi pham rgya mtsho.
KJ	*mKhas pa'i tshul la 'jug pa'i sgo*. 'Ju mi pham rgya mtsho.
KN	*rDzogs pa chen po mkha' 'gro snying thig gi khrid yig thar lam bgrod byed shing rta bzang po*. Nges don bstan 'dzin bzang po.
LW	*Light of Wisdom*. Vol. 2. Padmasambhava and Jamgön Kongtrül.
MV	*dBus dang mtha' rnam par 'byed pa'i bstan bcos kyi 'grel pa 'od zer phreng ba*. 'Ju mi pham rgya mtsho.
ND	*Lam zhugs kyi gang zag las dang po pa la phan pa'i bskyed rdzogs kyi gnad bsdus*. 'Jam mgon kong sprul blo gros mtha' yas.
NG	mTshams-brag Manuscript of the rNying ma rgyud 'bum.
NS	*The Nyingma School of Tibetan Buddhism*. Dudjom Rinpoche.
ON	*gSang 'grel phyogs bcu'i mun sel gyi spyi don 'od gsal snying po*. 'Ju mi pham rgya mtsho.

PK   Peking bka' 'gyur.

SG   *Theg pa lam zhugs kyi bshags pa'i rtsa 'grel bsdus pa thar lam sgron me*. Nges don bstan 'dzin bzang po.

ST   *Srog sdom gzer bzhi'i zin bris kun mkhyen brgyud pa'i zhal lung*. mKhan chen ngag dbang dpal bzang.

TC   *Theg pa'i mchog rin po che'i mdzod*. Klong chen rab 'byams.

TD   *Bod rgya tshig mdzod chen mo*. Krang dbyi sun, editor.

TK   *Shes bya kun khyab mdzod*. 'Jam mgon kong sprul blo gros mtha' yas.

TS   *rDzogs pa chen po gsang ba snying thig ma bu'i bka' srol chu bo gnyis 'dus kyi khrid yig dri med zhal lung*. Kong sprul blo gros mtha' yas.

WC   *Zab bsang bdud rtsi'i sgo 'byed skal bzang kun dga'i rol ston*. Dil mgo mkhyen brtse.

YD   *Theg pa chen po'i man ngag gi bstan bcos yid bzhin rin po che'i mdzod*. Klong chen rab 'byams.

YS   *sNying thig ya bzhi*. Klong chen rab 'byams, compiler.

YT   *Yon tan rin po che'i mdzod las 'bras bu'i theg pa'i rgya cher 'grel rnam mkhyen shing rta*. 'Jigs med gling pa.

ZD   *Zab don rgya mtsho'i sprin*. Klong chen rab 'byams.

Notes

FOREWORD

1. Patrul Orgyen Chokyi Wangpo (dPal sprul O rgyan chos kyi dbang po),
   Words of My Perfect Teacher (*rDzogs pa chen po klong chen snying thig gi
   sngon 'gro'i khrid yig kun bzang bla ma'i zhal lung*), in *dPal sprul O rgyan
   chos kyi dbang po'i gsung 'bum* (China: Si khron mi rigs dpe skrun khang,
   2003), vol. 7.
2. Longchen Rabjam (Klong chen rab 'byams), *Precious Wish-Fulfilling Treasury* (*Theg pa chen po'i man ngag gi bstan bcos yid bzhin rin po che'i mdzod*)
   (Gangtok, Sikkim: Sherab Gyaltsen and Khyentse Labrang, 1983).

TRANSLATOR'S INTRODUCTION

1. See Thupten Jinpa, ed., *Mind Training: The Great Collection* (Boston:
   Wisdom Publications, 2006) for an extraordinary compilation of mind-
   training texts.
2. Translated by the Lamrim Chenmo Translation Committee, 3 vols.
   (Ithaca, N.Y.: Snow Lion Publications, 2000–2004).
3. The main instructions for these practices are found in Patrul Rinpoche,
   Words of My Perfect Teacher (New Haven, Conn.: Yale University Press,
   2010) and Khenpo Ngawang Pelzang, *Guide to the Words of My Perfect
   Teacher* (Boston: Shambhala Publications, 2004).
4. These texts are contained in the companion volume to this publication,
   Cortland Dahl, ed., *Entrance to the Great Perfection* (Ithaca, N.Y.: Snow
   Lion Publications, 2009).
5. Both Jamyang Khyentse Wangpo's and Jamgön Kongtrul's instructions on
   the seven mind trainings are contained in the Heart Essence of Chetsün,
   the Chetsün Nyingtik. Further teachings by Jamgön Kongtrul can also
   be found in his commentary on the Heart Essence of the Karmapa, the
   Karma Nyingtik.
6. For an overview of the Fourfold Heart Essence and a distillation of its
   teachings, see Third Dzogchen Rinpoche, *Great Perfection: Outer and*

Inner Preliminaries (Ithaca, N.Y.: Snow Lion Publications, 2007) and Third Dzogchen Rinpoche, *Great Perfection*, Vol. 2, *Separation and Breakthrough* (Ithaca, N.Y.: Snow Lion Publications, 2008).

7. If you would like more background information on the lineage that gave birth to these teachings, you will find a concise history of the Nyingma lineage and its most important figures in Dahl, *Entrance to the Great Perfection*, along with an overview of the path of meditation taught in this approach. For a wonderful series of biographies of key lineage figures, I would recommend Tulku Thondup, *Masters of Meditation and Miracles* (Boston: Shambhala Publications, 1996), and if you are ready for a more in-depth take on the Nyingma lineage, its teachings, and its most illustrious figures, you will find no more thorough works than Dudjom Rinpoche, *The Nyingma School of Tibetan Buddhism* (Boston: Wisdom Publications, 1991) and Nyoshul Khenpo Jamyang Dorje, *A Marvelous Garland of Rare Gems* (Junction City, Calif.: Padma Publishing, 2005).

Excerpt from *The Tantra of the Sole Offspring*

1. *Tantra of the Sole Offspring* (*bsTan pa bu gcig gi rgyud gser gyi snying po nyi ma rab tu snang byed*), in *sNying thig ya bzhi*, 3:37–72.

Excerpt from *The Secret Commentary on the Tantra of the Sole Offspring*

1. *Garab Dorje's Secret Commentary on the Tantra of the Sole Offspring* (*bTags pas grol bar stan pa bu gcig gi gsang 'grel slob dpon dga' rab rdo rjes mdzad pa*), in *sNying thig ya bzhi*, 3:73–272.

The Steps to Liberation

1. In this verse, Jigme Lingpa is paying homage to Samantabhadra, the primordial buddha who is often equated with the very nature of mind and phenomena. Samantabhadra is also considered to be the original source of the Great Completion teachings and for this reason is the first figure mentioned in any discussion of the Dzogchen lineage. The six characteristics mentioned here refer to the way in which pure awareness (1) appears to itself, (2) emerges from the ground, (3) individuates, (4) is liberated through individuation, (5) does not occur from something other, and (6) abides in and of itself.

2. "Practicing the teachings to the letter" is an aphorism of the Kadampa

masters, who taught that all of the Buddha's teachings should be taken as practical advice. [TD 402]

3. An ancient unit of measurement; one hundred yojanas corresponds to 430 miles.

4. This refers to a Tibetan practice of creating molded figures, called *tsa-tsas*, of buddhas, stupas, and other sacred images as a means to generate merit.

IMPERMANENCE: THE FIRST MIND TRAINING

1. An epithet of Padmasambhava, Tötreng Tsal means "Powerful One [with the] Garland of Skulls."

SUFFERING AND COMPASSION: THE THIRD MIND TRAINING

1. These eight worldly concerns are pleasure and pain, gain and loss, praise and blame, and fame and infamy.

2. Author's note in the original text: As explained in *Elucidating the Significance of the Three Virtues.*

3. Author's note in the original text: The bracketed numbers shown here list the number of human years that equal one day in each of the god realms. Calculating their respective months and years, five hundred years in the Heaven of the Four Great Kings equals one day in the Reviving Hell. In order, one thousand years in the Heaven of the Thirty-Three, two thousand in the next heaven, then four, eight, and sixteen thousand years, equal one day in the Black Line Hell, the Crushing Hell, the Wailing Hell, the Great Wailing Hell, and the Inferno, respectively. As explained above, the life spans of the Great Inferno and the Hell of Incessant Torment are not calculated in this manner.

THE GURU: THE FOURTH MIND TRAINING

1. This line is most likely incorrect in Jigme Lingpa's text. In his Quintessence of the Dakinis, Longchenpa cites the same passage but renders this line "They are lax when it comes to vows, samaya, and practice" (*sdom dang dam tshig nyams len 'chal*). He also cites two further lines from the same tantra: "Do not teach the empowerments / And ultimate instructions of the Great Perfection / To a person who does not practice." [ZD 13] Here I have followed the version found in Longchenpa's writings.

2. The tale of Sadaprarudita is recounted in detail in Gampopa, *Jewel Ornament of Liberation* (Ithaca, N.Y.: Snow Lion Publications, 1998), 340–47.

3. This story can be found in Patrul Rinpoche, *Words of My Perfect Teacher*, 211–12.
4. Author's note in the original text: The four faults are the four misguided ideas that the guru is (1) not skilled in worldly activities, (2) younger than oneself, (3) one's spouse or relative, or (4) of lower status than oneself.
5. Two of the patriarchs of the Kagyü lineage, one of the four main lineages of Tibetan Buddhism. Naropa underwent many hardships while studying with Tilopa and is renowned for doing whatever his guru asked without hesitation.
6. A Tibetan colloquialism demonstrating a fickle mind.

Meditation: The Fifth Mind Training

1. This refers to the three great assemblies that followed in the centuries after the Buddha's death. At the first, the three baskets were compiled, with Ananda, due to his great memory, in charge of the Sutra Basket. It was also at this time that he first put all the teachings he had heard into practice; only later was he made a patriarch of the teachings, having attained the level of arhatship through practice.

Conclusion

1. In this stanza, Jigme Lingpa refers to two important collections of writings by Longchenpa.
2. An alternate name of Longchenpa that literally means "Pristine Light."
3. "Lake-Born Vajra" is one of many names applied to Padmasambhava.
4. An important commentary on *Resting in the Nature of Mind* (*Sems nyid ngal gso*) by Longchenpa.
5. Nyang Ral Nyima Özer (1124–92), an important tertön and previous incarnation of Jigme Lingpa.

Glossary

The following entries are translated excerpts from classical Buddhist texts. The bracketed information following each entry lists the abbreviated title and page number of the source text.

ABSOLUTE BODHICHITTA (*don dam byang sems*) – The wisdom that directly realizes EMPTINESS. [TD 1304]

ABSORPTION (*ting nge 'dzin*) – "To truly grasp," meaning that within this mental state one is able to focus one-pointedly and continuously on a given topic or on the object one is examining. [TD 1027]

ACCOMPLISHED MASTER (*grub thob*) – An individual who has actualized the unique realizations of the path and achieved both supreme and mundane SPIRITUAL ATTAINMENTS. [TD 403]

ACCUMULATION OF MERIT (*bsod nams kyi tshogs*) – The accumulation of positive, virtuous activities, such as making offerings, that involve a conceptual reference point. [TD 3051]

ACCUMULATION OF WISDOM (*ye shes kyi tshogs*) – The accumulation of nonreferential WISDOM is the accumulation of the undefiled VIRTUE that enacts the attainment of the DHARMAKAYA, the fruitional wisdom in which EMPTINESS is embraced by BODHICHITTA. [TD 2594]

ACTIVE WISDOM (*bya grub ye shes*) – The form of WISDOM that involves the enlightened form, speech, and mind spontaneously working for the welfare of sentient beings. [YT 431]

AFFLICTIONS (*nyon mongs pa*) – Factors that upset or disturb the mind and body and produce fatigue. [TD 971]

AKSHOBYA (Mi bskyod pa) – As one member of the FIVE BUDDHA FAMI-
LIES, Akshobya represents the vajra family and the principle of enlightened
mind, indivisible EMPTINESS and compassion. [BT 408]

AMITABHA ('Od dpag med) – As one member of the FIVE BUDDHA FAMI-
LIES, Amitabha represents the lotus family and the principle of enlightened
speech, the source of all the Buddhist teachings. [BT 408]

AMITAYUS (Tshe dpag med) – A buddha of the lotus family associated with
longevity.

AMOGHASIDDHI (Don yod grub pa) – As one member of the FIVE BUD-
DHA FAMILIES, Amoghasiddhi represents the karma family and the principle
of ENLIGHTENED ACTIVITY, which is carried out by venerating the buddhas
and working for the welfare of sentient beings. [BT 408]

AMRITA (*bdud rtsi*) – See NECTAR.

ANUTTARAYOGA TANTRA (*rNal 'byor bla na med pa'i rgyud*) – Literally,
"Unsurpassed Union Tantra." The fourth and highest of the FOUR CLASSES
OF TANTRA. In the NEW SCHOOLS, this system consists of the FATHER
TANTRA, MOTHER TANTRA, and NONDUAL TANTRA. In the NYINGMA
SCHOOL, this class of tantra is equated with the THREE INNER TANTRAS
of MAHAYOGA, ANUYOGA, and ATIYOGA. Ju Mipam explains the unique-
ness of this system: "From the perspective of this approach, not only is the
CAUSAL VEHICLE of the perfections a 'long path,' but the OUTER TANTRAS
are as well. In other words, this is the true 'swift path' and 'FRUITIONAL
VEHICLE.' All other approaches are taught according to the mind-sets of
disciples to lead them to this vehicle. Here, in contrast, the ultimate, DEFINI-
TIVE MEANING is revealed explicitly, just as it is seen by the WISDOM of the
BUDDHAS." [KG 37]

ANUYOGA (*rjes su rnal 'byor*) – Literally, "Concordant Yoga." Anuyoga
is the eighth of the NINE VEHICLES found in the tantric tradition of the
NYINGMA SCHOOL. To enter this system, one first receives the thirty-six
supreme EMPOWERMENTS, which include ten outer empowerments, eleven
inner empowerments, thirteen practice empowerments, and two SECRET
EMPOWERMENTS. Next, one trains in the Anuyoga view until one has come
to a definitive understanding of the essence of the threefold MANDALA of
SAMANTABHADRA. In the meditative system of this tradition, one practices

the paths of LIBERATION and SKILLFUL MEANS. The former involves settling in a nonconceptual state that is in harmony with REALITY itself or, in
accordance with letters, reciting MANTRAS to visualize a mandala of deities
(see YIDAM DEITY). The latter entails arousing coemergent WISDOM by relying upon the upper and lower gates. In terms of conduct, one understands all
appearances and mental events to be the play of the wisdom of great bliss, and
with this understanding, uses the direct cause of being beyond acceptance
and rejection to attain the fruition of this path. Here, the fruition involves
the five yogas (which are in essence the five paths), the completion of the ten
levels, and the attainment of the state of Samantabhadra. [TD 3120]

APPLICATION BODHICHITTA (*'jug pa'i byang chub kyi sems*) – To develop
BODHICHITTA by actually engaging in certain activities, such as the SIX PER-
FECTIONS, with the express aim of bringing all sentient beings to the state of
buddhahood. [TD 905] This consists of committing oneself to the cause of
enlightenment, in contrast to ASPIRATION BODHICHITTA, where one com-
mits oneself to its fruition. [YT 475]

APPLICATIONS OF MINDFULNESS (*dran pa nyer bzhag*) – "Mindfulness"
here refers to KNOWLEDGE of the characteristics of phenomena as they are,
unmistakenly. Hence, this aspect relates to INSIGHT. "Application" refers to
the placement of attention one-pointedly on the analytic process that one's
knowledge is engaged in. Hence, this aspect relates to TRANQUILITY. Most
commonly, there are said to be four applications of mindfulness, which are
the four focal points used when cultivating insight. These are (1) the application of mindfulness to the body, (2) the application of mindfulness to sensation, (3) the application of mindfulness to the mind, and (4) the application
of mindfulness to phenomena. These four partially constitute the THIRTY-
SEVEN FACTORS OF ENLIGHTENMENT. [TD 1322]

ASPIRATION BODHICHITTA (*smon pa'i byang chub kyi sems*) – To commit
oneself to attaining the fruitional [state of buddhahood], meaning that one is
oriented toward the attainment of enlightenment and, consequently, engages
in its related practices. [YT 475]

ATIYOGA (*Shin tu rnal 'byor*) – Literally, "Supreme Yoga." Atiyoga is the
highest of the NYINGMA tradition's NINE VEHICLES. In the textual tradition
of this tantric system, Atiyoga is equated with the GREAT PERFECTION of
one's self-occurring WISDOM. This wisdom is free from elaborations and not
subject to any sense of partiality or limitation. As such, it is considered the

very pinnacle of all the various vehicles, since it contains all of their significance. Within this Great Perfection, all the various phenomena of samsara
and nirvana, all that appears and exists, arise as the play of this self-occurring
wisdom, apart from which nothing exists. The fundamental basis of existence,
in this tradition, is this self-occurring wisdom. In terms of the path, there are
two forms of practice: the BREAKTHROUGH stage of original purity and the
DIRECT LEAP stage of spontaneous presence. Through these two practices,
the four visions are brought to a state of culmination, and one attains the
result of this process, liberation within the very ground, the attainment of the
permanent state of the YOUTHFUL VASE BODY. [TD 3118]

AVALOKITESHVARA (sPyan ras gzigs) – As a YIDAM DEITY, Avalokiteshvara is considered to be the unified essence of the enlightened speech of all
the BUDDHAS and the embodiment of compassion. [TD 1674]

AWARENESS MANTRA (*rig sngags*) – A MANTRA that is used to accomplish the activity of a DEITY and that emphasizes the VAJRA WISDOM of the
enlightened mind. [TD 2681]

BARDO (*bar do*) – See INTERMEDIATE STATE.

BLISSFUL ONE (*bde bar gshegs pa*) – An alternate term for a BUDDHA, who,
by relying upon the path of bliss—the VEHICLE OF THE BODHISATTVAS—
progresses to the blissful fruition, the state of perfect buddhahood. [TD
1368]

BODHICHITTA (*byang chub kyi sems*) – This mind-set comes about by taking
the welfare of others as one's focal point and then orienting oneself with the
desire to attain total and perfect enlightenment. This unique frame of mind
forms the core of the GREAT VEHICLE path. It can be divided into ASPIRA-
TION BODHICHITTA and APPLICATION BODHICHITTA. [TD 1869]

BODHISATTVA (*byang chub sems dpa'*) – Literally, "heroic being of enlightenment." Individuals who train in the GREAT VEHICLE and are so called
because they do not become discouraged in the face of the long duration it
takes to attain great enlightenment, nor do they hesitate in giving away their
own head and limbs out of generosity. [TD 1870]

BREAKTHROUGH (*khregs chod*) – Along with DIRECT LEAP, breakthrough
is one of two stages of practice found in the GREAT PERFECTION's KEY

INSTRUCTION CLASS. This practice is designed to liberate those prone to laziness in an effortless manner. In this approach, one first identifies, and then sustains recognition of, one's own innately pure, empty awareness. This practice is the essence of Great Perfection practice. [DZ 67]

BUDDHA (*sangs rgyas*) – One who has cleared away the darkness of the TWO OBSCURATIONS and in whom the two forms of KNOWLEDGE have blossomed. [TD 2913]

CAUSAL VEHICLE (*rGyu'i theg pa*) – An alternate name of the Vehicle of Characteristics, or Vehicle of Perfections, so-called because it takes the factors that cause the attainment of perfect buddhahood, such as the THIRTY-SEVEN FACTORS OF ENLIGHTENMENT, as the path. [TD 580]

CENTRAL CHANNEL (*rtsa dbu ma*) – The central channel is the main energetic channel in the body. It runs vertically through the center of the body. Its upper end is located at the cranial aperture on the crown of the head, while its lower end is found in the secret place (the perineum). [TD 2212]

CHAKRA (*'khor lo*) – (1) In terms of the energetic body, the chakras are circular conglomerations of energetic channels that are supported by the CENTRAL CHANNEL. [TD 2209] (2) As a symbolic implement used in DEVELOPMENT STAGE practice, the chakra is a circular instrument that symbolizes cutting through the AFFLICTIONS. [KR 51]

CHANNELS, ENERGIES, AND ESSENCES (*rtsa rlung thig le*) – These three factors function as the support for consciousness, ensuring that the life remains stable and the life-force uninterrupted. Of these three, the channels are said to be like a house, the essences like the wealth contained therein, and the ENERGIES like their owner. [TD 2213]

CHARYA TANTRA (*sPyod rgyud*) – Literally, "Performance Tantra." The second of the THREE OUTER TANTRAS; the view of this tradition is similar to that of YOGA TANTRA, while its conduct is equated with that of KRIYA TANTRA. For this reason, it is also known as "DUAL TANTRA." [NS 271] This is the second of the FOUR CLASSES OF TANTRA found in the NEW SCHOOLS.

CONDITIONED PHENOMENA (*'dus byas*) – That which has arisen or been constructed due to the coincidence of multiple causes and conditions; the phenomena that collectively constitute the five aggregates. [TD 1408]

DAKINI (*mkha' 'gro ma*) – (1) A yogini who has attained the extraordinary SPIRITUAL ATTAINMENTS, or (2) a female divinity who has taken birth in a PURE REALM or other similar location. [TD 298]

DEFINITIVE MEANING (*nges don*) – To specific disciples, it is taught that the profound nature of all phenomena is EMPTINESS—free from arising, cessation, and every other elaboration—and that the actual condition and nature of things is one of LUMINOSITY, which is beyond anything that can be thought or put into words. The definitive meaning refers to this nature, as well as to the scriptures that teach it and their related commentaries. [TD 655]

DEITY (*lha*) – See YIDAM DEITY.

DESIRE REALM (*'dod khams*) – One of the THREE REALMS that constitute SAMSARA; sentient beings in this realm are attached to material food and sex, primarily because they sustain themselves through the five sense pleasures. This realm is referred to as such because it is home to desirous sentient beings. [TD 1414]

DEVELOPMENT STAGE (*bskyed rim*) – Along with the completion stage, the development stage is one of two phases that constitute Buddhist practice in the THREE INNER TANTRAS. This form of practice purifies the habitual tendencies associated with the four types of birth by meditating on ordinary appearances, sounds, and thoughts as DEITY, MANTRA, and WISDOM. [TD 184] Explaining further, Ju Mipam writes, "The phases of development stage practice correspond to the way in which conventional existence develops. ... Practicing with this approach purifies the habitual patterns of SAMSARA, perfects the fruition of NIRVANA, and matures the practitioner for the completion stage." [ON 416] This practice is discussed extensively in DMW.

DHARMA (*chos*) – Most commonly, the word "dharma" is used to refer either to the Buddha's teachings or as a general term meaning "phenomena." As the Great Dictionary notes, however, this word has ten traditional usages, all of which relate to something that "holds its own essence." These ten are (1) knowable objects, (2) spiritual paths, (3) the transcendence of suffering, (4) mental objects, (5) merit, (6) life, (7) the sublime words of the Buddha, (8) temporal progression, (9) regulation, and (10) systems. [TD 825]

DHARMA PROTECTOR (*chos skyong*) – A protective DEITY that is bound under oath to protect the Buddhist teachings. [TD 830]

DHARMAKAYA (*chos kyi sku*) – One of the THREE KAYAS. When classified into two forms, the state of buddhahood is divided into the dharmakaya and RUPAKAYA, that is, the form of reality and the embodied forms. The dharmakaya benefits oneself and results from the culmination of abandonment and realization. [TD 829]

DIRECT LEAP (*thod rgal*) – Along with the BREAKTHROUGH stage, direct leap is one of two phases of practice found in the GREAT PERFECTION's KEY INSTRUCTION CLASS. In contrast to breakthrough, which focuses on emptiness and original purity, the direct leap emphasizes spontaneous presence and the active manifestations of reality itself. This approach is directed toward diligent individuals who liberate themselves through meditation. [YT 689]

DISCERNING WISDOM (*so sor rtogs pa'i ye shes*) – The inner state of clarity in which all that can be known is understood in a distinct manner. [ZD 78]

DISSOLUTION PHASE (*bsdu rim*) – A concluding ritual in which one dissolves the visualization of the DEVELOPMENT STAGE into the nonreferential sphere. [TD 1488]

DOMINANT RESULT (*bdag po'i 'bras bu*) – One of a fivefold classification of results; a result whose arising is entirely dictated by a particular cause that "dominates" its corresponding result, such as when virtuous activities cause a rebirth in a positive location. [TD 1358]

DUAL TANTRA (*gNyis ka rgyud*) – An alternate name for CHARYA TANTRA.

DZOGCHEN (*rDzogs chen*) – See GREAT PERFECTION.

EIGHT COLLECTIONS OF CONSCIOUSNESS (*rnam shes tshogs brgyad*) – The six collections of consciousness plus the afflicted mind and the all-ground consciousness. [TK 1, 50]

EKAJATI (E ka dza ti) – A wrathful female DHARMA PROTECTOR who safeguards the GREAT PERFECTION teachings.

EMPOWERMENT (*dbang*) – In a general sense, an empowerment is a tantric ritual that matures the student and allows her or him to engage in specific tantric practices. There are a great many divisions and descriptions pertaining to empowerment, such as those of the ground, path, and fruition. There are also unique empowerments associated with each tantric lineage and vehicle. Concerning the meaning of the term "empowerment," Jamgön Kongtrul explains that the original Sanskrit term has the literal meaning of "to scatter and pour." The meaning, he explains, is that empowerments cleanse and purify the psycho-physical continuum by "scattering" the obscurations and then "pouring" the potential of WISDOM into what is then a clean vessel, the purified psycho-physical continuum. [TK 3, 54] Stressing the importance of the empowerment ritual, Tsele Natsok Rangdröl writes, "Unless you first obtain the ripening empowerments, you are not authorized to hear even a single verse of the tantras, statements, and instructions. (Unauthorized) people who engage in expounding and listening to the tantras will not only fail to receive blessings, they will create immense demerit from divulging the secrets of these teachings. A person who has not obtained empowerment may pretend to practice the liberating instructions, but instead of bringing accomplishment, the practice will create obstacles and countless other defects." [EM 39]

EMPOWERMENT INTO THE DISPLAY OF AWARENESS (*rig pa'i rtsal dbang*) – In the ATIYOGA tradition, those with the fortune to do so may enter into the MANDALA of ultimate BODHICHITTA right from the beginning, without having to rely upon the symbolic wisdom of the first three empowerments. The empowerment that allows one to do so is the empowerment into the display of awareness. Quoting the master Manjushrimitra, Jamgön Kongtrul writes, "The profound, supreme, and true empowerment / Is the attainment of the empowerment into the display of awareness. / It is an empowerment because one realizes the nature of mind." [TK 3, 103]

EMPTINESS (*stong pa nyid*) – The manner in which all phenomena are devoid of inherent existence; their true nature. In certain contexts, sixteen or eighteen forms of emptiness are listed: (1) internal emptiness, (2) external emptiness, (3) internal and external emptiness, (4) the emptiness of emptiness, (5) great emptiness, (6) ultimate emptiness, (7) conditioned emptiness, (8) unconditioned emptiness, (9) emptiness that transcends extremes, (10) emptiness without beginning or end, (11) unrelinquished emptiness, (12) natural emptiness, (13) the emptiness of all phenomena, (14) the emptiness of particular characteristics, (15) unobservable emptiness, and (16) the emptiness of the essential lack of entities. When eighteen are listed, the following two are added: (17) the emptiness of the lack of entities, and (18) emptiness of the very essence. [TD 1110]

ENERGY (*rlung*) – One element of the triad ENERGIES, CHANNELS, AND ESSENCES. This factor has the nature of the five elements and completely pervades the energetic channels. [TD 2734]

ENLIGHTENED ACTIVITY (*'phrin las*) – One aspect of the fruitional state of buddhahood. The most common presentation of enlightened activity contains four divisions: pacifying, enriching, magnetizing, and wrathful activity. To these four, a fifth division is sometimes added, that of spontaneous activity. [TD 1771] According to Ju Mipam, enlightened activity can also be divided into supreme and mundane. The former, he writes, involves "planting the seed of liberation in the minds of others by granting EMPOWERMENTS, and through MANTRAS, MUDRAS, and so forth, while the latter functions to bring others more temporary forms of happiness." [ON 559]

ESSENCE KAYA (*ngo bo nyid sku*) – As discussed in the Perfection of Knowledge literature, the essence kaya is one particular facet of buddhahood. In particular, this refers to the kaya of the perfection of the SPHERE OF REALITY, in which there are two forms of purity: natural purity and incidental purity. [TD 663]

FAITH (*dad pa*) – Generally, three types of faith are discussed in the scholastic tradition: lucid faith, inspired faith, and the faith of conviction. The first entails a lucid frame of mind that arises in reference to the Three Jewels. The second concerns the desire to engage the third and fourth noble truths and reject the first two noble truths (suffering and its source). The third involves having conviction in the principle of karmic causality. [YD 607]

FATHER TANTRA (*Pha rgyud*) – The Father Tantra emphasizes both the methods of the DEVELOPMENT STAGE and the energetic practices of the completion stage. In the NEW SCHOOLS, the Father Tantra includes the five stages of the *Guhyasamaja Tantra*. [ST 6] In the NYINGMA SCHOOL, the Father Tantra is equated with MAHAYOGA, the seventh of the NINE VEHICLES. [DZ 24]

FIVE ACTS OF IMMEDIATE RETRIBUTION (*mtshams med lnga*) – (1) To kill one's father, (2) to kill one's mother, (3) to kill a FOE-DESTROYER, (4) to create a schism within the Buddhist community, and (5) to maliciously draw blood from the body of a BUDDHA. [TD 2311]

FIVE BUDDHA FAMILIES (*rigs lnga*) – The five buddha families function as the support for the FIVE WISDOMS. The relationship between these two groups is as follows: The WISDOM OF THE SPHERE OF REALITY is linked with the buddha family and the buddha VAIROCHANA, ACTIVE WISDOM with the karma family and the buddha AMOGHASIDDHI, the WISDOM OF EQUALITY with the jewel family and the buddha Ratnasambhava, DISCERNING WISDOM with the lotus family and the buddha AMITABHA, and MIRROR-LIKE WISDOM with the VAJRA family and either VAJRASATTVA or AKSHOBYA. [TK 2, 80]

FIVE PERFECTIONS (*phun sum tshogs pa lnga*) – The perfect teaching, the perfect time, the perfect teacher, the perfect place, and the perfect retinue. [TD 1718]

FIVE WISDOMS (*ye shes lnga*) – According to Jigme Lingpa, wisdom can be divided into twenty-five categories, as there are five different forms of wisdom present in each continuum of the FIVE BUDDHA FAMILIES. [YT 431] More commonly, however, five forms of wisdom are taught. Dudjom Rinpoche explains that the WISDOM OF THE SPHERE OF REALITY is that which realizes how things really are, whereas the four subsequent wisdoms—MIRROR-LIKE WISDOM, the WISDOM OF EQUALITY, DISCERNING WISDOM, and ACTIVE WISDOM—in their function of supporting and depending upon the former, constitute the wisdom that comprehends all that exists. It has also been explained that the first wisdom mentioned above refers to the ultimate, while the latter four relate to the relative. [NS 140]

FOE-DESTROYER (*dgra bcom pa*) – One who has destroyed or conquered all of his or her foes, here referring to the four demons. [TD 464] This is the fruition of the FOUNDATIONAL VEHICLE.

FORM REALM (*gzugs khams*) – The abodes of the first through fourth states of ABSORPTION, which are located in the space above Mount Meru. The inhabitants of this realm have bodies of light that are clear by nature. Although they are free from passion, they still cling to form. [TD 2499]

FORMLESS REALM (*gzugs med khams*) – The four spheres of perception, from that of boundless space up to the peak of existence. In these spheres, there is no coarse form, only clear mental forms. The beings in these realms are free of attachment to form but are attached to the state of formlessness. [TD 2503]

FOUNDATIONAL VEHICLE (*Theg pa dman pa*) – The vehicle of the LISTEN-ERS and SOLITARY BUDDHAS. [TD 1183] See also SUTRA VEHICLE, VEHI-CLE OF THE LISTENERS, AND VEHICLE OF THE SOLITARY BUDDHAS.

FOUR AGGREGATES (*phung po bzhi*) – The four psychological aggregates that, along with a fifth aggregate of form, serve as the basis for the belief in a self. These four are sensation, perception, conditioned formations, and consciousness.

FOUR CLASSES OF TANTRA (*rgyud sde bzhi*) – The four classes of tantra are KRIYA TANTRA, CHARYA TANTRA, YOGA TANTRA, and ANUTTARA-YOGA TANTRA. These four divisions are commonly presented in the NEW SCHOOLS and subsume all tantric teachings. Although this classification system is also found in the NYINGMA SCHOOL, that tradition more often groups the tantras into the THREE OUTER TANTRAS and the THREE INNER TANTRAS.

FOUR ELEMENTS (*'byung ba bzhi*) – The four elements that comprise the physical body: the earth element, water element, fire element, and air element. [TD 1982]

FOUR EMPOWERMENTS (*dbang bzhi*) – The VASE EMPOWERMENT, SECRET EMPOWERMENT, KNOWLEDGE-WISDOM EMPOWERMENT, and PRECIOUS WORD EMPOWERMENT. [TD 1935]

FOUR FORMS OF FEARLNESSNESS (*mi 'jigs pa bzhi*) – (1) Fearlessness in the face of perfect realization, (2) fearlessness in the face of perfect abandon-ment, (3) fearlessness in the face of teaching obstructive phenomena, and (4) fearlessness in the face of teaching the path of certain release. [TD 2068]

FOUR IMMEASURABLES (*tshad med bzhi*) – Immeasurable love, immeasur-able compassion, immeasurable joy, and immeasurable equanimity; these four mind-sets are held by practitioners of the GREAT VEHICLE and are so called because one meditates by focusing on sentient beings without any sense of limitation, and because they bring an immeasurable amount of merit. [TD 2260]

FOUR ROOT CHAKRAS (*rtsa gnas 'khor lo bzhi*) – As visualized in the SECRET MANTRA, the radial channels that project outward from the three primary energetic channels: the thirty-two channels that comprise the chakra of great bliss at the crown, the sixteen channels that comprise the chakra of enjoyment at the throat, the eight channels that comprise the dharma chakra in the heart center, and the sixty-four channels that comprise the emanation chakra in the navel area. [TD 2209]

FOURFOLD HEART ESSENCE (sNying thig ya bzhi) – A collection of GREAT PERFECTION teachings compiled by Longchen Rabjam. This compilation contains five primary divisions: (1) the HEART ESSENCE OF THE DAKINIS (Khandro Nyingtik), the Dzogchen teachings of PADMASAMBHAVA; (2) the Quintessence of the Dakinis (Khandro Yangtik), a collection of Longchenpa's commentaries on Padmasambhava's teachings; (3) the HEART ESSENCE OF VIMALAMITRA (Vima Nyingtik), the Dzogchen teachings of Vimalamitra; (4) the Quintessence of the Guru (Lama Yangtik), a collection of Longchenpa's commentaries on Vimalamitra's teachings; and (5) the Profound Quintessence (Zabmo Nyingtik), a collection of Longchenpa's commentaries that apply to both Padmasambhava's and Vimalamitra's teachings.

FRUITIONAL VEHICLE (*'Bras bu'i theg pa*) – An alternate term for the VAJRA VEHICLE. Ju Mipam explains, "This vehicle is referred to as such because the essential fruition is seen to be present within the very ground, whereas in other systems it is believed to be something that must be attained. Hence, in this system, the fruition is taken as the path in the present moment." [KG 40]

GLORIOUS MAGICAL WEB (*sGyu 'phrul drva ba*) – See TANTRA OF THE SECRET ESSENCE.

GREAT COMPASSIONATE ONE (Thugs rje chen po) – Mahakaruna; a form of the BODHISATTVA AVALOKITESHVARA.

GREAT PERFECTION (*rDzogs pa chen po*) – This term is used in the tantric tradition of the NYINGMA SCHOOL, where it refers to the DHARMAKAYA (the nature of the mind lacking an essence), the SAMBHOGAKAYA (self-illumination), and the NIRMANAKAYA (pervasive compassionate resonance). Thus, in the Great Perfection, all the qualities of the THREE KAYAS are spontaneously perfect, and since this is the way all phenomena really are, it is great. [TD 2360]

GREAT VEHICLE (*theg pa chen po*) – The VEHICLE OF THE BODHISATTVAS, so called because it is superior to the FOUNDATIONAL VEHICLE of the LISTENERS and SOLITARY BUDDHAS in seven ways. [TD 1183]

GROUND, PATH, AND FRUITION (*gzhi lam 'bras gsum*) – The view, meditation, and result of each vehicle. The ground consists of coming to a definitive understanding of the view; the path involves familiarizing oneself with this through meditation; and the fruition is the attainment of enlightenment. [TD 2421]

GUHYAGARBHA TANTRA (*rGyud gsang ba snying po*) – See ***TANTRA OF THE SECRET ESSENCE***.

GURU (*bla ma*) – A teacher. According to *Clarifying the Practice of the Heart Essence*, there are three types of guru: (1) the external guru, who introduces one to meanings and the symbols that represent them, (2) the inner guru of understanding and experiencing the way things are, and (3) the secret, true guru of realization. The text goes on to explain, "for the novice practitioner, the outer guru is of paramount importance." [HE 16]

GURU YOGA (*bla ma'i rnal 'byor*) – A meditative ritual in which the practitioner meditates on his or her root guru as the union of all the buddhas. [TD 1914]

HEART ESSENCE (sNying thig) – The KEY INSTRUCTION CLASS of the GREAT PERFECTION contains various divisions, the most profound of which is termed Nyingtik, or Heart Essence. In the Heart Essence, the first stage of practice is the BREAKTHROUGH of original purity, or *kadak trekchö*. *Kadak* is original purity, meaning the primordially pure nature of awareness. "Breakthrough" refers to the process resolving the nature of emptiness by breaking past or cutting through all levels of conceptuality, even the experiences of meditation. The second stage of practice is called the DIRECT LEAP into spontaneous presence, or *lhundrup tögal*. This term conveys the sense of leaping straight into the immediate experience of original wisdom. Here, the quality of vivid clarity is emphasized, the spontaneously present, luminous nature of mind. This phase is likened to crossing over a mountain pass directly, rather than climbing in a more methodic, step-by-step manner. [GP2 xviii]

HEART ESSENCE OF THE DAKINIS (mKha' 'gro snying thig) – A collection of instructions from the NYINGMA SCHOOL that the master PADMASAMBHAVA directly taught the DAKINI Yeshe Tsogyal and which were subsequently revealed as a TREASURE by Pema Ledrel Tsel. [TD 297] This is one division of the FOURFOLD HEART ESSENCE, a collection of GREAT PERFECTION instructions compiled by the master Longchenpa.

HEART ESSENCE OF THE VAST EXPANSE (Klong chen snying thig) – The mind TREASURE of Rigdzin Jigme Lingpa. [TD 48]

HEART ESSENCE OF VIMALAMITRA (Bi ma'i snying thig) – The GREAT PERFECTION teachings of Vimalamitra, which were compiled by Long-chenpa and included in the FOURFOLD HEART ESSENCE.

HERUKA (*he ru ka*) – (1) A blood drinker, (2) Chakrasamvara, or (3) a general name for wrathful deities. [TD 3069]

HINAYANA (*Theg pa dman pa*) – See FOUNDATIONAL VEHICLE.

INDIVIDUAL LIBERATION (*so sor thar pa*) – The liberation from the lower realms and samsara that those who maintain discipline [practitioners of the FOUNDATIONAL VEHICLE] attain for themselves. [TD 2959]

INNER TANTRAS (*nang rgyud*) – See THREE INNER TANTRAS.

INSIGHT (*lhag mthong*) – Along with TRANQUILITY, insight is one of the common denominators and causes of all states of ABSORPTION. It entails the observation of the specific distinguishing nature of a given object. [TD 3092]

INTERDEPENDENT ORIGINATION (*rten 'brel*) – The fact that all phenomena arise due to the interdependent relationship of their own specific causes and conditions. [KJ 18] See also TWELVE LINKS OF INTERDEPENDENT ORIGINATION.

INTERMEDIATE STATE (*bar srid/bar do*) – The bardo, or intermediate state, typically refers to the state that occurs between death and a future rebirth. It can also, however, refer to the transitional periods that constitute the entire stream of existence, inclusive of birth, dreaming, meditation, death, REALITY itself, and transmigration. Concerning the specific completion stage practice that relates to this state, Dza Patrul writes (referring to the three intermediate states of death, reality itself, and transmigration): "In the first intermediate state, one brings LUMINOSITY onto the path as the DHARMAKAYA. In the second, union is brought onto the path as SAMBHOGAKAYA. And in the third, rebirth is taken onto the path as NIRMANAKAYA." [DR 445]

KADAMPA SCHOOL (*bKa' gdams pa*) – A Buddhist school founded by Atisha and Dromtön that believed that each and every teaching of the Buddha should be understood as a practical instruction. [TD 72]

KAMA (*bka' ma*) – See TRANSMITTED TEACHINGS OF THE NYINGMA SCHOOL.

KARMA (*las*) – The nature of action; a mental factor that propels the mind toward a concordant object and causes it to fluctuate. [TD 2769] See also PRINCIPLE OF KARMIC CAUSALITY.

KAYA (*sku*) – An honorific term for body, which is often used to refer to the "body" or "form" of buddhahood, in all its various aspects. See also NIR-MANAKAYA, SAMBHOGAKAYA, DHARMAKAYA, and ESSENCE KAYA.

KEY INSTRUCTION CLASS (*Man ngag sde*) – The third and most profound division of the GREAT PERFECTION teachings, along with the MIND CLASS and SPACE CLASS. This category is further divided into outer, inner, secret, and extremely secret unsurpassed cycles. The latter refers to the HEART ESSENCE teachings of the Great Perfection. This refers primarily to the HEART ESSENCE OF THE DAKINIS (the key instructions that were taught by the master of Oddiyana, PADMASAMBHAVA) and the HEART ESSENCE OF VIMALAMITRA (the lineage of the great scholar Vimalamitra). [TD 2056] See also THREE CLASSES OF THE GREAT PERFECTION.

KHANDRO NYINGTIK (Mkha' 'gro snying thig) – See HEART ESSENCE OF THE DAKINIS.

KNOWLEDGE (*shes rab*) – Knowledge is the factor that focuses on a specific entity, examines this object, and is then able to distinguish its essence and individual features, its general and specific characteristics, and whether it should be taken up or abandoned. Once perfected, it functions to dispel doubt. "Knowledge" is synonymous with the terms "total awareness," "total understanding," "awakening," "thorough analysis," "thorough understanding," "confidence," "intellect," "mental functioning," and "clear realization." [TD 2863]

KNOWLEDGE-WISDOM EMPOWERMENT (*shes rab ye shes kyi dbang*) – The second of the three higher, supreme EMPOWERMENTS, which is bestowed upon the student's mind in dependence upon the MANDALA of the female MUDRA. This purifies mental impurities and, in terms of the path, empowers the student to train in the completion stage. As the result of this empowerment, a causal link is formed that leads to the attainment of the DHARMA-KAYA. [TD 2865]

KRIYA TANTRA (*Bya rgyud*) – Literally, "Activity Tantra." First of the THREE OUTER TANTRAS. The view of this system, in terms of the ultimate, relates to the self-purity of all phenomena, while, relatively, one gains SPIRITUAL ATTAINMENTS by being blessed by the pure DEITY. Practice in this tradition focuses on the WISDOM BEING and MANTRA recitation. Its conduct involves various forms of ritual purification and asceticism. [KG 34]

LIBERATION (*thar pa*) – To be freed from that which binds; in terms of samsara, that which binds is KARMA and the AFFLICTIONS. Hence, these are the factors that need to be eliminated for liberation to occur. Synonyms for "liberation" include "freedom," "true goodness," "immortality," "the ultimate," "the immaculate," "complete freedom," "elimination," "purity and freedom," "enlightenment," "NIRVANA," "peace," and "the absence of rebirth." [TD 1153]

LISTENER (*nyan thos*) – An individual who has entered into the VEHICLE OF THE LISTENERS, one of the THREE VEHICLES. These are individuals who do not focus on practicing the teachings associated with the GREAT VEHICLE but are so called because they "listen" or hear the teachings from the Buddha and so forth, and then repeat what they have heard to others. Hence they are also known as "those who listen and then repeat." [TD 933]

LONGCHEN NYINGTIK (Klong chen snying thig) – See HEART ESSENCE OF THE VAST EXPANSE.

LOWER EXISTENCE (*ngan 'gro*) – A general term used to refer to the three lower realms, where beings experience nothing but intense suffering as the result of the great number of nonvirtuous acts they committed in the past. [TD 646]

LOWER REALM (*ngan song*) – Synonymous with LOWER EXISTENCE. [TD 649]

LUMINOSITY (*'od gsal*) – Though the term "luminosity" literally means "light that is able to dispel darkness" [TD 2535], it is also commonly used in reference to WISDOM, the subjective counterpart to REALITY. As the practitioner progresses along the various paths and levels, the manner in which luminous wisdom perceives its object, REALITY, becomes more and more refined. [NO 4, 17]

MAGICAL WEB (*sGyu 'phrul drva ba*) – See *TANTRA OF THE SECRET ESSENCE*.

MAHAMUDRA (*Phyag rgya chen po*) – (1) "Mahamudra" is the term given to the ultimate fruition, the supreme spiritual accomplishment. (2) The term can also refer to one of the four MUDRAS taught in the YOGA TANTRA tradition. In this context, the practice of Mahamudra relates to the enlightened form. As such, it eliminates the temporary confusion of the all-ground consciousness and actualizes its nature, MIRROR-LIKE WISDOM. [TD 1732] Also a fruitional teaching of the Kagyü and Geluk schools that emphasizes the nature of mind.

MAHAYANA (*Theg pa chen po*) – See GREAT VEHICLE.

MAHAYOGA (*rNal 'byor chen po*) – Mahayoga is one of NINE VEHICLES found in the Nyingma tantric tradition. In this system, one begins by maturing one's state of being with the eighteen supreme EMPOWERMENTS: the ten outer, beneficial empowerments; the five inner empowerments of potentiality; and the three profound, secret empowerments. In the next step, one comes to a definitive understanding of the view, which relates to the indivisibility of the superior two truths. In terms of meditation, the DEVELOPMENT STAGE is emphasized—the three ABSORPTIONS form the structure for this stage of practice, while its essence consists of a threefold process: purification, perfection, and maturation. This is then sealed with the four stakes that bind the life-force. In the completion stage practice of this system, one meditates on the CHANNELS, ENERGIES, and ESSENCES and LUMINOSITY. Then, as the conduct, one relies upon the direct cause, which can be either elaborate in form, unelaborate, or extremely unelaborate, and then attains the fruition of this process—the completion of the five paths (which are subsumed under the four MASTERS OF AWARENESS). This state of fruition is known as the unified state of the VAJRA HOLDER. [TD 2052]

MANDALA (*dkyil 'khor*) – Explaining the meaning of this term, Ju Mipam writes, "*Manda* means 'essence,' or 'pith,' while *la* has the sense of 'to take,' or 'grasp.' Hence, together this term means 'that which forms the basis for grasping essential qualities.' Alternately, when this word is translated literally as a whole, it means 'that which is wholly spherical and entirely surrounds.'"
Concerning the various types of mandala, Mipam continues, "There are three types of mandala: those of the ground, path, and fruition. The natural

mandala of the ground refers to the universe and its inhabitants being primordially present as divinities, both in terms of the support and supported. . . . In terms of the path, there is the mandala of meditation, of which there are two forms: the symbolic mandala (such as paintings, lines, arrangements, and those made from colored powder) and the true mandala that is represented by these forms (enlightened form, speech, and mind). . . . The mandala of the ultimate fruition is composed of the enlightened forms and WISDOMS that occur once the path has been completely traversed and one has attained the state of SAMANTABHADRA." [ON 494] The term "threefold mandala" refers to the physical mandala of the DEITY, the verbal mandala of MANTRA, and the mental mandala of concentration. [KN 94]

MANJUGHOSHA ('Jam dpal gzhon nur gyur pa) – The "Gentle, Glorious, and Youthful One." See also MANJUSHRI.

MANJUSHRI ('Jam dpal dbyangs) – The "Gentle, Glorious, and Melodic One"; a BODHISATTVA and YIDAM DEITY that personifies perfect knowledge. He is "gentle" in the sense of having totally eliminated any trace of coarse negativity and glorious in that he is in the form of a sixteen-year-old youth at all times. [TD 888]

MANTRA (*sngags*) – Mantras are formations of syllables that protect practitioners of the VAJRA VEHICLE from the ordinary perceptions of their own minds. They also function to invoke the YIDAM DEITIES and their retinues. [TD 707] Explaining the etymology of the term, Dudjom Rinpoche writes, "*Mana*, which conveys the meaning of mind, and *traya*, which conveys that of protection, become 'mantra' by syllabic contraction, and therefrom the sense of protecting the mind is derived." [NS 257] See also SECRET MANTRA VEHICLE.

MARKS AND SIGNS (*mtshan dpe*) – The excellent marks and signs that signify a fully realized being. [TD 2306]

MASTER OF AWARENESS (*rig pa 'dzin pa*) – In this term, "awareness" refers to DEITY, MANTRA, and the WISDOM of great bliss. One who has "mastered" these three with profound and SKILLFUL MEANS is a "master of awareness." [TD 2683]

MASTER OF AWARENESS OF THE GREAT SEAL (*phyag rgya chen po rig 'dzin*) – One of the four MASTERS OF AWARENESS, four levels of SPIRITUAL

ATTAINMENT that present the progression through the paths and levels of SECRET MANTRA in the NYINGMA SCHOOL. This classification subsumes the path of cultivation, referring to the form of wisdom that occurs on the unified path of training once one has arisen from the luminosity of the path of seeing. [TD 1733]

MASTER OF AWARENESS WITH POWER OVER LONGEVITY (*tshe dbang rig 'dzin*) – One of the four MASTERS OF AWARENESS, four levels of SPIRITUAL ATTAINMENT that present the progression through the paths and levels of SECRET MANTRA in the NYINGMA SCHOOL. This level of attainment occurs on the path of seeing, where the support present in the supreme state transforms into a clear, vajra-like body, while the mind matures into the wisdom of the path of seeing and, as a result, one attains a state of freedom from birth and death. [TD 2282]

MATURED MASTER OF AWARENESS (*rnam smin rig 'dzin*) – One of the four MASTERS OF AWARENESS, four levels of SPIRITUAL ATTAINMENT that present the progression through the paths and levels of SECRET MANTRA in the NYINGMA SCHOOL. This level of attainment occurs on the path of seeing, where one first gains stability in the DEVELOPMENT STAGE. Though the mind itself matures into its divine form at this point, the residual elements are not able to be purified. [TD 1574] See also MASTER OF AWARENESS.

MEDITATION (*sgom pa*) – See VIEW, MEDITATION, CONDUCT, AND FRUITION.

MIDDLE WAY (*dBu ma*) – A body of literature and a philosophical school that teaches profound emptiness. [TD 1939]

MIND CLASS (*Sems sde*) – See THREE CLASSES OF THE GREAT PERFECTION.

MIND LINEAGE OF THE VICTORIOUS ONES (*rgyal ba dgongs brgyud*) – In this lineage, the victorious one SAMANTABHADRA transmits realization to the regents of the FIVE BUDDHA FAMILIES. These five, in turn, transmit this realization to their simultaneously arisen retinue, the BODHISATTVAS and so forth. [SD 69]

MIRROR-LIKE WISDOM (*me long lta bu'i ye shes*) – An aspect of WISDOM, its self-illumination and unobstructed capacity to manifest. [ZD 78]

MOTHER TANTRA (*Ma rgyud*) – In the Mother Tantra, the completion stage associated with the subtle essences is emphasized, in which case one relies upon either the body of another or one's own body. In the NEW SCHOOLS, the Mother Tantra includes Naropa's Six Dharmas. [ST 6] In the NYINGMA SCHOOL, the Mother Tantra is equated with ANUYOGA, the eighth of the NINE VEHICLES. [DZ 24]

MUDRA (*phyag rgya*) – Most commonly, the term "seal," or "mudra," refers to physical gestures that embody certain Buddhist principles. According to Ju Mipam, however, the Sanskrit term "mudra" carries the meaning of "a stamp, symbol, or seal that is difficult to move beyond." Explaining further, he writes, "What this means is that these are unique factors that symbolize the enlightened form, speech, mind, and activities of realized beings. Once something has been 'sealed' with one of these, it is difficult to stray from the factor that is being represented." [ON 568]

NECTAR (*bdud rtsi*) – A substance that allows one to conquer death. [TD 1362]

NEW SCHOOLS (*gSar ma*) – This appellation is applied most commonly to the Sakya, Kagyü, and Geluk traditions. More specifically, it refers to those who uphold the tantras of the SECRET MANTRA that were brought to Tibet in a period that began with the work of the great translator Rinchen Zangpo (tenth century CE). [TD 3008] See also NYINGMA SCHOOL.

NGÖNDRO (*sngon 'gro*) – See PRELIMINARY PRACTICE.

NINE VEHICLES (*theg pa dgu*) – The nine vehicles constitute the path of the Ancient Translation School, the NYINGMA SCHOOL, or Ngagyur Nyingma. The first three vehicles are those of the SUTRA VEHICLE, the exoteric Buddhist teachings: (1) the VEHICLE OF THE LISTENERS, (2) the VEHICLE OF THE SOLITARY BUDDHAS, and (3) the VEHICLE OF THE BODHISATTVAS. The next set constitutes the THREE OUTER TANTRAS: (4) the Vehicle of KRIYA TANTRA, or Activity Tantra; (5) the Vehicle of Ubhaya Tantra, or DUAL TANTRA; and (6) the Vehicle of YOGA TANTRA, or Union Tantra. The final set of three represents the inner tantric tradition: (7) the Vehicle of MAHAYOGA, or Great Yoga; (8) the Vehicle of ANUYOGA, or Concordant Yoga; and (9) the Vehicle of ATIYOGA, or Supreme Yoga (also known as the GREAT PERFECTION). [NS 164]

NIRMANAKAYA (*sprul pa'i sku*) – (1) A form of buddhahood that arises from the empowering condition of the SAMBHOGAKAYA; an embodied form that comes into existence and appears to both pure and impure disciples, working for the benefit of these beings in accordance with their mental predispositions. (2) A name applied to the reincarnations of great lamas. [TD 1689]

NIRVANA (*mya ngan las 'das pa*) – (1) LIBERATION from suffering, or (2) peace. [TD 2126]

NONDUAL TANTRA (*gNyis med rgyud*) – The third of three divisions that constitute the ANUTTARAYOGA TANTRA; Nondual Tantra stresses the view of the path of LIBERATION. In the NEW SCHOOLS, this includes the Six Applications of the *Kalachakra Tantra*. [ST 6]

NYINGMA SCHOOL (*rNying ma'i lugs*) – This tradition, which consists of NINE VEHICLES, is also referred to as the SECRET MANTRA School of the Early Translations. The teachings of this school were first translated into Tibetan during the eighth-century reign of King Trisong Deutsen and spread by the master PADMASAMBHAVA and his followers. [TD 992]

NYINGTIK (*sNying thig*) – See HEART ESSENCE.

NYINGTIK YABSHI (*sNying thig ya bzhi*) – See FOURFOLD HEART ESSENCE.

OATH-BOUND PROTECTORS (*dam can*) – Worldly protective spirits that have taken a sacred oath [to safeguard the Buddha's teachings]. [TD 1245]

OUTER TANTRAS (*phyi rgyud*) – See THREE OUTER TANTRAS.

PADMASAMBHAVA (Pad ma 'byung gnas) – An alternate name of Guru Rinpoche, the Indian Buddhist master who was one of the primary figures who brought Buddhism to Tibet in the eighth century CE and whose teachings are the basis for the NYINGMA SCHOOL.

PERFORMANCE TANTRA (*sPyod rgyud*) – See CHARYA TANTRA.

PRECIOUS WORD EMPOWERMENT (*tshig dbang rin po che*) – The precious word EMPOWERMENT is one of the three higher supreme empowerments.

This is bestowed upon the student's ordinary body, speech, and mind in reliance upon the MANDALA of ultimate BODHICHITTA. It purifies the impurities associated with the THREE GATES, along with their related habitual patterns. In terms of the path, it empowers the student to train in the natural GREAT PERFECTION. As its result, a causal link is formed that leads to the attainment of the ESSENCE KAYA, VAJRA WISDOM. [TD 2271]

PRELIMINARY PRACTICE (*sngon 'gro*) – An activity that must be completed prior to beginning the main practice. [TD 716]

PRINCIPLE OF KARMIC CAUSALITY (*las rgyu 'bras*) – The causes and results associated with virtuous and negative actions, such as the fact that suffering results from engaging in negative activities. [TD 2773]

PURE PERCEPTION (*dag snang*) – The perception that all that appears and exists, the entire universe and its inhabitants, is a PURE REALM and the play of the KAYAS and WISDOM. [TD 1237]

PURE REALM (*zhing khams*) – A pure land where BUDDHAS and BODHISATTVAS abide, such as the Realm of Bliss. [TD 2388]

RAINBOW BODY (*'ja' lus*) – The LIBERATION of the physical body into a body of light. [TD 892]

REALITY (*chos nyid*) – (1) The character or nature of something, or (2) the empty nature of things. [TD 836]

REFUGE (GOING FOR) (*skyabs 'gro*) – To rely upon and supplicate one's GURU and the THREE JEWELS, placing one's faith and trust in them, in order to be protected from temporary and ultimate fears and suffering. [TD 142]

RELATIVE BODHICHITTA (*kun rdzob byang chub kyi sems*) – All forms of BODHICHITTA that arise from coarse conceptual designations. [TD 24]

RENUNCIATION (*nges 'byung*) – The desire to be free from all planes of SAMSARA, liberated from the prison of the THREE REALMS, and delivered to the blissful state of NIRVANA. [TD 658]

RICHLY ARRAYED REALM (*sTug po bkod pa'i zhing*) – A SAMBHOGAKAYA realm located above the seventeen levels of the FORM REALM. [TD 1103]

RIPENED RESULT (*rnam smin gyi 'bras bu*) – One division of a fivefold classification of results; a result that emerges from the ripening of either defiled VIRTUE or vice, such as the defiled, perpetuating aggregates. [TD 1574]

RUPAKAYA (*gzugs kyi sku*) – This refers to the NIRMANAKAYA, the emanated form that has attachment, and the SAMBHOGAKAYA, the form of perfect enjoyment that does not. These KAYAS manifest in an embodied manner for the benefit of others. They appear to the perception of impure and pure disciples, respectively, once the referential ACCUMULATION OF MERIT has been perfected. [TD 2499]

SADHANA (*sgrub pa/sgrub thabs*) – As Ju Mipam explains, a sadhana is "that which enables one to attain or accomplish a desired end." In terms of tantric practice, he writes, this refers to "all the various practices that utilize the unique methods of the SECRET MANTRA tradition to achieve whatever SPIRITUAL ATTAINMENTS one desires, whether supreme or mundane." [ON 534]

SAKYA SCHOOL (*Sa skya*) – A Buddhist lineage established in Tibet by Khön Könchok Gyalpo. [TD 2889]

SAMANTABHADRA (Kun tu bzang po) – (1) That which is virtuous and good in every way, completely perfect; (2) the SPHERE OF REALITY, the DHARMAKAYA; (3) a general term for buddhahood; (4) a particular TATAGATA; (5) a particular BODHISATTVA; and (6) the SAMBHOGAKAYA of the Bön tradition. [TD 18]

SAMANTABHADRI (Kun tu bzang mo) – The female counterpart of SAMANTABHADRA. Representing WISDOM, Samantabhadri embodies the empty nature of all phenomena, the "pure spacious expanse." [NS 284]

SAMAYA VOWS (*dam tshig*) – Along with the vows of INDIVIDUAL LIBERATION found in the FOUNDATIONAL VEHICLE and the BODHISATTVA precepts of the GREAT VEHICLE, the samaya vows are one of three sets of vows that form the basis for Buddhist practice. These vows are associated specifically with the VAJRAYANA. Jamgön Kongtrul explains, "The word *samaya* means 'pledged commitment,' 'oath,' 'precept,' and so forth. Hence, this refers to a vajra promise or samaya because one is not to transgress what has been pledged. Samaya vows involve both benefit and risk because if kept, samaya vows become the foundation for all the trainings of MANTRA. If not kept, however, all these trainings become futile." There are innumerable divisions of the samaya vows found in the various tantras. At the most fundamental level, however, one pledges to continually maintain the view of the enlightened form, speech, and mind of the buddhas. [LW 46]

SAMBHOGAKAYA (*longs spyod rdzogs pa'i sku*) – One of the five KAYAS. While not wavering from the DHARMAKAYA, this form appears solely to those disciples who are noble BODHISATTVAS. It is also the basis for the arising of the NIRMANAKAYA and is adorned with MARKS AND SIGNS. [TD 2818]

SAMSARA (*'khor ba*) – Literally, to revolve in a cyclic manner; the abode of the six classes of existence or, said differently, the five defiled and perpetuating aggregates. [TD 316]

SARMA SCHOOLS (*gSar ma*) – See NEW SCHOOLS.

SECRET EMPOWERMENT (*gsang dbang*) – The secret EMPOWERMENT is the first of the three higher supreme empowerments (the other two being the KNOWLEDGE-WISDOM EMPOWERMENT and the PRECIOUS WORD EMPOWERMENT). This is bestowed upon the ordinary speech of the student by relying upon the MANDALA of relative BODHICHITTA of the male and female partners in union. This purifies the impurities of ordinary speech. In terms of the path, this empowers one to meditate on the energetic practices and recite MANTRA. In terms of the fruition, a link is formed to the attainment of the SAMBHOGAKAYA and VAJRA SPEECH. [TD 3006]

SECRET MANTRA (*gSang sngags*) – Secret Mantra is the WISDOM of great bliss, which protects the mind from subtle concepts through the union of empty KNOWLEDGE and compassionate SKILLFUL MEANS. It is referred to as such because it is practiced in secret and not divulged to those who are not suitable recipients of these teachings. [TD 3002] See also SECRET MANTRA VEHICLE.

SECRET MANTRA VEHICLE (*gSang sngags kyi theg pa*) – An alternate term for the VAJRA VEHICLE. Ju Mipam explains, "This system is 'secret' insofar as the profound MANDALA of the victorious ones' enlightened form, speech, and mind is present as the innate nature of all phenomena. Nevertheless, this is inherently hidden from those who are confused and must be revealed skillfully. It is not revealed explicitly to the inferior practitioners of the lower approaches but is transmitted secretly. Hence, it is not part of the range of experience of ordinary disciples. The term 'MANTRA' indicates that, in order to practice the mandala of these three secrets, this nature is presented as it actually is; it is not hidden or kept secret." [KG 38]

SELFLESSNESS (*bdag med*) – See TWOFOLD SELFLESSNESS.

SELF-OCCURRING WISDOM (*rang byung ye shes*) – The primordial indwelling awareness present within the mind-streams of all sentient beings, the indivisibility of space and wisdom. [TD 2650]

SEVEN ASPECTS OF UNION (*kha sbyor yan lag bdun*) – The nature of a SAMBHOGAKAYA BUDDHA possesses these seven aspects of union: (1) complete enjoyment, (2) union, (3) great bliss, (4) absence of nature, (5) being completely filled with compassion, (6) being uninterrupted, and (7) being unceasing. [TD 204]

SEVEN MIND TRAININGS (*sems sbyong don bdun ma*) – A unique teaching from the Secret HEART ESSENCE, which allows those unable to directly perceive the appearances of awareness to avoid the pitfall of mistrusting the Heart Essence teachings, and to gradually perceive their own awareness. The seven points of this system are: (1) impermanence, (2) short-term and long-lasting happiness, (3) manifold circumstances, (4) the pointlessness of worldly activities, (5) the qualities of the BUDDHA, (6) the GURU's key instructions, and (7) nonconceptuality. [TS 134–35] Not to be confused with the seven-point mind training of Atisha (*blo sbyong don bdun*), a contemplative system that stems from the KADAMPA SCHOOL.

SHRAVAKA (*nyan thos*) – See LISTENER.

SIDDHA (*grub thob*) – See ACCOMPLISHED MASTER.

SIX CLASSES OF SENTIENT BEINGS (*'gro ba rigs drug*) – The six classes of beings found within cyclic existence: gods, demigods, humans, animals, hungry ghosts, and hell beings. [TD 518]

SIX LINEAGES (*brgyud pa drug*) – The six lineages of the TRANSMITTED TEACHINGS OF THE NYINGMA SCHOOL and TREASURES. This includes the three lineages that are common to both the Transmitted Teachings and the treasure tradition: (1) the lineage of the victors' realization, (2) the symbolic lineage of the MASTERS OF AWARENESS, and (3) the hearing lineage of people, as well as three additional lineages that relate specifically to the karmically linked treasures: (4) the lineage of transmissions and prophecies,

(5) the lineage of aspirations and empowerments, and (6) the lineage entrusted to DAKINIS. [NS 745] In Longchenpa's *A Cloud on the Ocean of Profound Reality*, the lineage of transmissions and prophecies is referred to as "the lineage of compassionate blessings." [ZD 308]

SIX ORNAMENTS (*rgyan drug*) – Six great Buddhist masters from ancient India: the two ornaments of the Middle Way: Nagarjuna and Aryadeva; the two ornaments of the Abhidharma: Asanga and Vasubhandu; and the two ornaments of Pramana: Dignaga and Dharmakirti. [TD 545]

SIX PERFECTIONS (*pha rol tu phyin pa drug*) – (1) Generosity, (2) discipline, (3) patience, (4) diligence, (5) ABSORPTION, and (6) KNOWLEDGE. [TD 1698]

SKILLFUL MEANS (*thabs*) – An activity that enables one to accomplish a given outcome easily. [TD 1148] See also VEHICLE OF SKILLFUL MEANS.

SOLITARY BUDDHA (*rang sangs rgyas*) – These beings, in their final existence, do not rely upon a master. Instead, they analyze the REALITY of INTERDEPENDENT ORIGINATION and, on that basis, realize the selflessness of the individual as well as half of the selflessness of phenomena. In so doing, they become FOE-DESTROYERS who have achieved the actualization of solitary enlightenment. [TD 2659] See also FOUNDATIONAL VEHICLE.

SPACE CLASS (*Klong sde*) – See THREE CLASSES OF THE GREAT PERFECTION.

SPHERE OF REALITY (*chos kyi dbyings*) – (1) EMPTINESS, or (2) the empty nature of the five aggregates. [TD 840]

SPIRITUAL ATTAINMENT (*dngos grub*) – The positive result that one aims to attain by practicing a particular set of spiritual instructions. [TD 675]

SPONTANEOUSLY PRESENT MASTER OF AWARENESS (*lhun grub rig 'dzin*) – One of the four MASTERS OF AWARENESS, four levels of SPIRITUAL ATTAINMENT that constitute the NYINGMA SCHOOL's approach of progressing through the paths and levels of SECRET MANTRA. This classification refers to the path beyond training and the attainment of the ultimate fruition, the spontaneous presence of the five KAYAS—the state of a VAJRA HOLDER. [TD 3107]

SUGATA (*bde bar gshegs pa*) – See BLISSFUL ONE.

SUPREME VEHICLE (*Theg mchog*) – An epithet of the GREAT PERFECTION, or ATIYOGA, the ninth of the NYINGMA SCHOOL'S NINE VEHICLES.

SUTRA (*mdo*) – See SUTRA VEHICLE.

SUTRA VEHICLE (*mDo'i theg pa*) – The Buddhist teachings are often classified into two divisions, which represent two approaches to enlightenment—the Sutra Vehicle and the VAJRA VEHICLE. The former is often referred to as the "Causal Vehicle" because, in this tradition, practice consists of assembling the causes that lead to the attainment of liberation. This vehicle is further divided into the VEHICLE OF THE LISTENERS and the VEHICLE OF THE SOLITARY BUDDHAS (which together constitute the FOUNDATIONAL VEHICLE) and the VEHICLE OF THE BODHISATTVAS (the GREAT VEHICLE).

SVABHAVIKAKAYA (*ngo bo nyid sku*) – See ESSENCE KAYA.

TANTRA (*rgyud*) – (1) A continuum that remains temporally unbroken, (2) a thread, (3) a region or district, (4) bloodline, or (5) the SECRET MANTRA and its related texts. [TD 573]

TANTRA OF THE SECRET ESSENCE (*rGyud gsang ba snying po*) – This text, often referred to as the *Guhyagarbha Tantra*, is the most widely studied tantra in the NYINGMA SCHOOL. It was translated by Vimalamitra, Nyak Jnanakumara, and Ma Rinchen Chok. The full title of this twenty-two-chapter text is *Tantra of the True Nature of Reality: The Glorious Secret Essence*. [TD 574] While this tantra is most often linked with the MAHAYOGA tradition, it is also listed as an ANUYOGA tantra in certain contexts and an ATIYOGA tantra in others, which is due to the fact that the view of this set of literature is said to correspond to that of Atiyoga, while in terms of conduct it is linked with Mahayoga. According to Ju Mipam, it is fine to classify this text as belonging to any one of the THREE INNER TANTRAS, from the perspective of emphasizing its teachings on the DEVELOPMENT STAGE, the completion stage, or the GREAT PERFECTION, respectively. [KG 10]

TARA (*sGrol ma*) – A female YIDAM DEITY whose name (literally, "the Liberator") signifies her capacity to liberate beings from the eight forms of fear. [TD 625]

TATAGATA (*de bzhin gshegs pa*) – An epithet of the BUDDHAS, referring to one who, in dependence upon the path of REALITY, abides in neither existence nor peace and has passed into the state of great enlightenment. [TD 1287]

TEN GROUNDS (*sa bcu*) – The ten stages of awakening that mark the culmination of the bodhisattva path.

TEN POWERS (*stobs bcu*) – The ten powers of the BUDDHAS: (1) the power to know the correct and incorrect; (2) the power to know the ripening of karma; (3) the power to know the variety of individual interests; (4) the power to know the variety of individual characters; (5) the power to know both superior and inferior faculties; (6) the power to know all paths that can be traveled; (7) the power to know the meditative concentrations of total liberation, absorption, stability, and so on; (8) the power to know previous births; (9) the power to know of death, transmigration, and rebirth; and (10) the power to know of the exhaustion of defilements. [TD 1119]

TERMA (*gter ma*) – See TREASURE.

TERTÖN (*gter ston*) – One who reveals a terma, or TREASURE. [TD 1048]

THIRTY-SEVEN FACTORS OF ENLIGHTENMENT (*byang phyogs so bdun*) – The thirty-seven factors of enlightenment are qualities that occur at various stages of the Buddhist path. According to Maitreya's *Distinguishing the Middle from Extremes*, these are (1–4) the four APPLICATIONS OF MINDFULNESS that occur on the lesser path of accumulation; (5–8) the four authentic eliminations that occur on the intermediate path of accumulation; (9–12) the four bases of miraculous power that occur on the greater path of accumulation; (13–17) the five faculties that occur on the first two stages of the path of connection—the stages of heat and summit; (18–22) the five powers that occur on the last two stages of the path of connection—the stage of acceptance and the supreme state; (23–29) the seven aspects of enlightenment that occur on the path of knowledge; and (30–37) the eightfold noble path that occurs on the path of cultivation. [MV 732]

THIRTY-TWO MARKS OF THE BUDDHAS (*mtshan bzang po so gnyis*) – See MARKS AND SIGNS.

THODGAL (*thod rgal*) – See DIRECT LEAP.

THREE CLASSES OF THE GREAT PERFECTION (*rdzogs chen sde gsum*) – According to Longchenpa, the first transmission of the GREAT PERFECTION teachings in the human realm took place between Garab Dorje and Manjushrimitra. The former passed on his teachings in the form of 6,400,000 verses. The latter then codified his master's teachings and divided them into three categories: the MIND CLASS, SPACE CLASS, and KEY INSTRUCTION CLASS. [TC 16] Explaining these three categories, Jigme Lingpa writes, "There are no phenomena that exist apart from one's very own mind. Therefore, one is freed from the idea that there are things that need to be rejected. This is the Mind Class. In addition, all forms of phenomenal existence have nowhere to go other than REALITY itself—the expanse of SAMANTABHADRI. Because of this, one is freed from the extreme of needing antidotes. This is the activity-free Space Class. Finally, the profound Key Instruction Class involves being liberated from both factors that need to be rejected and antidotes by arriving at a decisive certainty concerning the true nature of things." [YT 608]

THREE COLLECTIONS (*sde snod gsum*) – The three collections are a vehicle used to express the entire range of teachings given by the Buddha. The VINAYA COLLECTION, the Sutra Collection, and the Abhidharma Collection each relate to one of the THREE TRAININGS: those of discipline, meditation, and KNOWLEDGE, respectively. These three contain all the words and meanings found within the twelvefold collection of sacred Buddhist writings and encompass all the various topics that can be known, from form all the way up to omniscience. [TD 1473]

THREE GATES (*sgo gsum*) – Body, speech, and mind. [TD 595]

THREE INNER TANTRAS (*nang rgyud gsum*) – In the textual tradition of the NYINGMA SCHOOL, the three inner tantras constitute the final three of this tradition's NINE VEHICLES. They are listed as the tantras of MAHAYOGA, the scriptures of ANUYOGA, and the key instructions of ATIYOGA. [TD 1505] These three divisions are also associated with the practices of the DEVELOPMENT STAGE, the completion stage, and the GREAT PERFECTION. As Dilgo Khyentse explains, "Development and Mahayoga are like the basis for all the teachings, completion and Anuyoga are like the path of all the teachings, and the Great Perfection of Atiyoga is like the result of all the teachings." [WC 773]

THREE JEWELS (*dkon mchog gsum*) – The BUDDHA, DHARMA, and Sangha. [TD 61]

THREE KAYAS (*sku gsum*) – The DHARMAKAYA, SAMBHOGAKAYA, and NIRMANAKAYA. [TD 125]

THREE OUTER TANTRAS (*phyi rgyud gsum*) – In the textual tradition of the NYINGMA SCHOOL, the three outer tantras are listed as KRIYA TANTRA (Activity Tantra), CHARYA TANTRA (Performance Tantra), and YOGA TANTRA (Union Tantra). These traditions are also referred to as the "Vedic Vehicles of Ascetic Practice," due to the fact that they include various ascetic practices, such as ritual cleansing and purification, that are similar to those found in the Vedic tradition of the Hindu Brahmin caste. [TD 1740]

THREE REALMS (*khams gsum*) – The DESIRE, FORM, and FORMLESS REALMS. [TD 226]

THREE ROOTS (*rtsa gsum*) – The three roots are the three inner objects of REFUGE: the GURU, YIDAM DEITY, and DAKINI. A guru is a qualified teacher who has liberated his or her own mind and is skilled in the methods that tame the minds of others. The yidam deities are the vast array of peaceful and wrathful deities and those associated with the Eight Great Sadhana Teachings. The dakinis are those associated with the three abodes. The latter refers to VAJRAVARAHI in particular, the divine mother who gives birth to all BUDDHAS. [KN 23]

THREE SPHERES (*'khor gsum*) – Agent, act, and object. [TD 320]

THREE TRAININGS (*bslab pa gsum*) – (1) Discipline, (2) concentration, and (3) KNOWLEDGE. [TD 3056]

THREE VAJRAS (*rdo rje gsum*) – VAJRA BODY, VAJRA SPEECH, and VAJRA MIND.

THREE VEHICLES (*theg pa gsum*) – The VEHICLE OF THE LISTENERS, the VEHICLE OF THE SOLITARY BUDDHAS, and the VEHICLE OF THE BODHISATTVAS. [TD 1183]

TORMA (*gtor ma*) – Torma is one of the primary offerings found in the SECRET MANTRA tradition, where, along with medicine and blood, it constitutes the inner offerings. Though there are various divisions of torma, the outer torma offering consists of "the choicest types of edibles heaped upon a vessel of precious substances," which, as Jamgön Kongtrul explains, embodies "the indivisibility of the SPHERE OF REALITY and WISDOM." [LW 129] Explaining the significance of torma in different contexts, Dilgo Khyentse writes, "Generally speaking, torma should be viewed as the MANDALA in the context of approach and accomplishment, as sense pleasures in the context of making offerings, as the DEITY in the context of EMPOWERMENT, and as the SPIRITUAL ATTAINMENTS at the conclusion of a practice." [WC 743]

TRANQUILITY (*zhi gnas*) – One of the common denominators and causes of all states of ABSORPTION. This form of meditation involves settling the mind one-pointedly in order to pacify the mind's tendency to be distracted outward to external objects. [TD 2384]

TRANSMITTED TEACHINGS OF THE NYINGMA SCHOOL (*rNying ma bka' ma*) – The teachings of the NYINGMA SCHOOL have been transmitted through two lineages: the distant lineage of the Transmitted Teachings and the close lineage of the TREASURES. In the former, the teachings of MAHAYOGA, ANUYOGA, and ATIYOGA are preserved, respectively, under the headings of the *Tantra of the Magical Net*, the *Sutra of the Condensed Realization*, and MIND CLASS. [NS 396]

TREASURE (*gter ma*) – The teachings of the NYINGMA SCHOOL have been transmitted through two lineages: the distant lineage of the TRANSMITTED TEACHINGS OF THE NYINGMA SCHOOL and the close lineage of the treasures. In the latter, the teachings that are passed on consist of three primary categories: those that relate to Guru PADMASAMBHAVA, the GREAT PERFECTION, and the GREAT COMPASSIONATE ONE, AVALOKITESHVARA. [NS 396]

TWELVE ASCETIC VIRTUES (*sbyangs pa'i yon tan bcu gnyis*) – (1) Wearing cast-off clothing, (2) wearing only three Dharma robes, (3) wearing woolen garments, (4) eating only one meal a day, (5) begging for alms, (6) not eating after noon, (7) staying in isolated places, (8) staying at the foot of trees, (9) living in exposed places, (10) staying in charnel grounds, (11) sleeping only while sitting up, and (12) staying wherever one finds oneself. [TD 2023]

TWELVE LINKS OF INTERDEPENDENT ORIGINATION (*rten 'brel yan lag bcu gnyis*) – The internal process of interdependent origination, that is, the twelve links of interdependent origination that relate to the emergence of the sentient beings that inhabit the universe. These twelve consist of the three links that propel, the four links that are propelled, the three links that are to be established, and the two links that are established. [TD 1075]

TWENTY-FIVE DISCIPLES (*rje 'bangs nyer lnga*) – The twenty-five ACCOMPLISHED MASTERS to whom PADMASAMBHAVA transmitted many VAJRA VEHICLE teachings. This occurred during the reign of King Trisong Deutsen, who invited Padmasambhava to Tibet. The twenty-five disciples are (1) King Trisong Deutsen, (2) Namkhai Nyingpo, (3) Sangye Yeshe, (4) Gyalwa Chokyang, (5) Yeshe Tsogyal, (6) Palgyi Yeshe, (7) Palgyi Senge, (8) Berotsana, (9) Nyak Jnanakumara, (10) Yudra Nyingpo, (11) Dorje Dudjom, (12) Yeshe Yang, (13) Sokpo Lhapel, (14) Shang Yeshe De, (15) Palgyi Wangchuk, (16) Denma Tsemang, (17) Kawa Peltsek, (18) Shupu Palgyi Senge, (19) Gyalwe Lodrö, (20) Kyeu Chung Lotsawa, (21) Otren Palgyi Wangchuk, (22) Ma Rinchen Chok, (23) Lhalung Palgyi Dorje, (24) Langdro Konchok Jungne, and (25) Lasum Gyalwa Changchup. [TD 910]

TWO ACCUMULATIONS (*tshogs gnyis*) – The ACCUMULATION OF MERIT and the ACCUMULATION OF WISDOM. The first of these involves a conceptual reference point and consists of wholesome endeavors, such as acts of generosity. [TD 3051] The second is the accumulation of nonreferential WISDOM, which refers to the accumulation of the undefiled VIRTUE that enacts the attainment of the DHARMAKAYA, the fruitional wisdom in which EMPTINESS is embraced by BODHICHITTA. [TD 2594]

TWO FORMS OF WISDOM (*ye shes gnyis*) – The wisdoms of meditative equipoise and postmeditation. [TD 2595]

TWO OBSCURATIONS (*sgrib pa gnyis*) – The afflictive obscurations and cognitive obscurations. [TD 612]

TWOFOLD BENEFIT (*don gnyis*) – One's own benefit and that of others. [TD 1302]

TWOFOLD SELFLESSNESS (*bdag med gnyis*) – The selflessness of the individual and the selflessness of phenomena. [TD 1358]

UNEXCELLED YOGA (*rNal 'byor bla na med pa*) – See ANUTTARAYOGA TANTRA.

VAIROCHANA (rNam par snang mdzad) – As one member of the FIVE BUD-DHA FAMILIES, Vairochana represents the buddha family of enlightened form, the foundation of all positive qualities. [BT 408]

VAJRA (*rdo rje*) – (1) That which is unchanging and indestructible, (2) an ancient Indian symbol that represents skillful means in the pairing of SKILL-FUL MEANS and KNOWLEDGE, (3) one of the twenty-seven coincidences in Tibetan astrology, or (4) an abbreviation of the Tibetan word for "diamond." [TD 1438] In VAJRAYANA practice, this symbolic implement is associated with a number of important principles. Generally speaking, it is linked with the male principle, compassion, skillful means, and the great bliss of unchang-ing REALITY. [YT 671]

VAJRA BODY (*sku rdo rje*) – As one of the THREE VAJRAS, the vajra body is the KAYA of indivisible appearance and EMPTINESS—the purification of ordinary form. [TD 122]

VAJRA HELL (*rDo rje dmyal ba*) – A term used in the SECRET MANTRA tradition to refer to the Hell of Incessant Torment. [TD 1442]

VAJRA HOLDER (*rdo rje 'dzin pa*) – (1) Great VAJRADHARA, (2) VAJRA-PANI, (3) a master of the SECRET MANTRA, or (4) Indra. [TD 1440]

VAJRA MASTER (*rdo rje slob dpon*) – A vajra master is a GURU who either grants EMPOWERMENT into a MANDALA of the SECRET MANTRA or teaches its liberating instructions. [TD 1442]

VAJRA MIND (*thugs rdo rje*) – One of the THREE VAJRAS. According to Jamgön Kongtrul, vajra mind is linked with the DHARMAKAYA and the union of bliss and EMPTINESS. [LW 37]

VAJRA SPEECH (*gsung rdo rje*) – One of the THREE VAJRAS. According to Jamgön Kongtrul, vajra speech is linked with the SAMBHOGAKAYA and the union of LUMINOSITY and EMPTINESS. [LW 36]

VAJRA VEHICLE (*rDo rje theg pa*) – Following the FOUNDATIONAL VEHI-CLE and the GREAT VEHICLE, the Vajra Vehicle is the third and highest vehicle in the Buddhist tradition. In particular, it contains the teachings on Buddhist TANTRA. Ju Mipam explains the significance of this appellation, "In this system, one does not accept or reject illusory, relative phenomena. Instead, the relative and ultimate are engaged as an indivisible unity and one's own three gates are linked with the nature of the THREE VAJRAS. Therefore, this vehicle is "vajra-like" insofar as these elements are seen to be indivisible and the very embodiment of primordial enlightenment, in which there is nothing to accept or reject, hence the term 'Vajra Vehicle.'" [KG 39] See also VEHICLE OF SKILLFUL MEANS, FRUITIONAL VEHICLE, and SECRET MANTRA VEHICLE.

VAJRA WISDOM (*ye shes rdo rje*) – Vajra wisdom is linked with the SVABHA-VIKAKAYA and the union of awareness and EMPTINESS. [LW 36]

VAJRADHARA (rDo rje 'chang) – Vajradhara is considered to be the sovereign lord of all buddha families and the teacher of the TANTRAS. It is also said that this is the form Shakyamuni took when teaching the SECRET MAN-TRA. [TD 1439]

VAJRAKILAYA (rDo rje phur pa) – A YIDAM DEITY associated with the principle of enlightened activity from the Eight Great Sadhana Teachings.

VAJRAKUMARA (rDo rje gzhon nu) – A YIDAM DEITY of the ANUTTARA-YOGA TANTRA; another name for VAJRAKILAYA. [TD 1440]

VAJRAPANI (Phyag na rdo rje) – Vajrapani is the condensation of the enlightened mind of all the BUDDHAS and the embodiment of their strength, might, and power. [TD 1734]

VAJRASADDHU (rDo rje legs pa) – A wrathful male Dharma protector who safeguards the GREAT PERFECTION teachings.

VAJRASATTVA (rDo rje sems dpa') – Vajrasattva is a YIDAM DEITY who is considered to be the sovereign lord of the hundred buddha families. He is white in appearance and sits in the vajra posture. With his right hand, he holds a VAJRA at his heart, and with his left, a bell at his hip. He is closely associated with purification. [TD 1442]

VAJRAVARAHI (rDo rje phag mo) – Literally, "Indestructible Sow." A semi-wrathful female YIDAM DEITY, the female counterpart of Chakrasamvara ('Khor lo bde mchog). [TD 1440] The divine mother who gives birth to all BUDDHAS. [KN 23]

VAJRAYANA (*rDo rje theg pa*) – See VAJRA VEHICLE.

VASE EMPOWERMENT (*bum dbang*) – The vase empowerment is a maturing EMPOWERMENT that is common to both the OUTER TANTRAS and the THREE INNER TANTRAS. In the latter, a MANDALA (either one made from colored powders or painted on canvas) is used to bestow the various subdivisions of this empowerment upon the student. This includes the water, crown, and other sections. This process purifies physical impurities and, in terms of the path, empowers one to practice the DEVELOPMENT STAGE. In terms of fruition, a causal link is formed that leads to the attainment of the VAJRA BODY—the NIRMANAKAYA. [TD 853, 2865]

VEHICLE OF SKILLFUL MEANS (*Thabs kyi theg pa*) – An alternate term for the VAJRA VEHICLE. Ju Mipam explains the significance of this appellation, "This approach is referred to as such due to the four characteristics of its SKILLFUL MEANS, which are great, easy, many, and swift. With the key points of this path, afflictive and pure phenomena are not engaged from the perspective of needing to be accepted or rejected. As this is the case, they do not obscure. In addition, its methods are great, insofar as they lead to the perfection of the TWO ACCUMULATIONS. In other systems, such skillful means do not exist." [KG 38]

VEHICLE OF THE BODHISATTVAS (*Byang chub sems dpa'i theg pa*) – This vehicle is first entered by taking the vows of ASPIRATION BODHICHITTA and APPLICATION BODHICHITTA. Its view involves realizing the TWOFOLD SELFLESSNESS, while its meditation consists of meditating on the THIRTY-SEVEN FACTORS OF ENLIGHTENMENT. Its conduct consists of training in the four ways of attracting students and the SIX PERFECTIONS. The fruition of this vehicle is twofold: on a temporary level, there are ten levels that are attained, while its ultimate fruition is the attainment of the level of universal illumination [the state of buddhahood]. [TD 1874] See also BODHISATTVA, GREAT VEHICLE, and SUTRA VEHICLE.

VEHICLE OF THE LISTENERS (*Nyan thos kyi theg pa*) – In this vehicle, one starts out by agreeing to adhere to one of the seven types of discipline associated with the vows of INDIVIDUAL LIBERATION and to keep this discipline from degenerating. In terms of the view, one recognizes that all the phenomena included within the five aggregates are devoid of a personal self, yet one still holds to the idea that the two subtle, indivisible phenomenal selves truly exist. One's meditation consists of TRANQUILITY and INSIGHT, the former referring to the nine ways to settle the mind and the latter to meditating on the sixteen aspects of the four noble truths. In terms of conduct, one maintains the TWELVE ASCETIC VIRTUES. The fruition of this vehicle entails attaining the levels of the stream-enterer, the once-returner, the nonreturner, and the FOE-DESTROYER. Each of these contains two further divisions—abiding and remaining—making eight in total. [TD 933] See also LISTENER and SUTRA VEHICLE.

VEHICLE OF THE SOLITARY BUDDHAS (*Rang sangs rgyas kyi theg pa*) – On this path, one realizes the character of INTERDEPENDENT ORIGINATION, both in its normal progression and also in reverse order, doing so without relying upon a teacher. This realization brings about a realization of the selflessness of the individual and the elimination of afflictive obscurations. [TD 2659] See also SOLITARY BUDDHA and SUTRA VEHICLE.

VIDHYA MANTRA (*rigs sngags*) – One of three types of MANTRA. Vidhya, or KNOWLEDGE, mantras are used primarily to accomplish the enlightened activities of a DEITY and the aspect of knowledge, VAJRA MIND. [TD 2681]

VIEW, MEDITATION, CONDUCT, AND FRUITION (*lta spyod sgom 'bras*) – These four factors comprise the various elements involved in Buddhist practice. Jamgön Kongtrul explains, "Though there are a great many divisions when it comes to view, meditation, and conduct, they can all be applied to the individual mind. The view is absolute conviction in its actual nature, while meditation means to apply this to one's own state of being. Conduct involves linking whatever arises with this view and meditation, and finally, the fruition is the actualization of the true nature of reality." [ND 6]

VIMA NYINGTIK (Bi ma'i snying thig) – See HEART ESSENCE OF VIMALAMITRA.

VINAYA COLLECTION (*'Dul ba'i sde snod*) – One section of a threefold division that constitutes the Buddhist teachings; this scriptural division emphasizes the training of supreme discipline. [TD 1407]

VIRTUE (*dge ba*) – The opposite of negativity; positive endeavors or good conduct; a phenomenon that is classified as having a definite mode of maturation, insofar as its result is [always] pleasant. [TD 450]

WISDOM (*ye shes*) – Inborn knowing; the empty and clear awareness that is self-occurring within the mind-streams of all sentient beings. [TD 2593]

WISDOM OF EQUALITY (*mnyam nyid ye shes*) – The aspect of WISDOM in which one internalizes the fact that all phenomena are equal, in the sense that they are all devoid of characteristics. [YT 431]

WISDOM OF THE SPHERE OF REALITY (*chos dbyings ye shes*) – The aspect of WISDOM that is empty in essence and unchanging. [ZD 78]

YIDAM DEITY (*yi dam*) – Yidams are the deities, BUDDHAS, and BODHI-SATTVAS that form the unique support for tantric practice. [TD 2565] Concerning the ultimate nature of the yidam deity, Jigme Lingpa writes, "You must realize that it is your own mind, with its EIGHT COLLECTIONS OF CONSCIOUSNESS, that arises as the KAYAS and WISDOM of the deity." [JL 235] This topic is discussed extensively in DMW.

YOGA TANTRA (*rNal 'byor rgyud*) – Yoga Tantra is the last of the THREE OUTER TANTRAS. In this system, emphasis is placed on the internal process of ABSORPTION. In terms of the path, there are two forms of practice: the practice of SKILLFUL MEANS and the practice of KNOWLEDGE. In the first, one practices DEITY yoga in conjunction with the four MUDRAS. In the latter, one realizes the inner REALITY of the mind and actualizes DISCERNING WISDOM. To supplement this internal process, external forms of ritual purification are also practiced. [SG 335]

YOGA VEHICLE (*Yo ga'i theg pa*) – See YOGA TANTRA.

YOGI(NI) (*rNal 'byor pa/ma*) – A male/female practitioner of a spiritual path. [TD 1579]

YOUTHFUL VASE BODY (*gzhon nu bum sku*) – "Youthful vase body" is a concept unique to the tradition of the Great Perfection. It refers to the realization of SAMANTABHADRA, the identity of which encompasses the ocean of WISDOMS and KAYAS and possesses six particular characteristics. These six refer to the external illumination of consciousness turning inward and the state of inner illumination that follows. The inner illumination of the great, primordial ground and space of being (1) manifests in its own natural state, (2) emerges from the ground, (3) is differentiated, (4) is liberated through differentiation, (5) does not come from somewhere else, and (6) remains in its own place. [TD 2432]

ZA RAHULA (Gza' ra hu la) – A wrathful male Dharma protector who safeguards the GREAT PERFECTION teachings.

Works Cited

Application of Mindfulness Sutra. (*'Phags pa dam pa'i chos dran pa nye bar bzhag pa; Arya saddharmanusmrtyupasthana*). DK: 0287, mdo sde, ya.

Buddha Avatamsaka Sutra (*Sangs rgyas phal po che zhes bya ba shin tu rgyas pa chen po'i mdo; Buddha avatamsaka nama mahavaipulya sutra*). DK: 0044, phal chen, ka-a.

Condensation (*sDud pa*). See *Sutra That Condenses the Precious Qualities of Realized Beings.*

Delineation of Karma (*Las rnam par 'byed pa; Karmavibhanga*). DK: 0338, mdo sde, sa.

Dharani of the Jewel Lamp (*'Phags pa dkon mchog ta la la'i gzungs zhes bya ba theg pa chen po'i mdo; Arya ratnolka nama dharani mahayana sutra*). DK: 0847, gzungs, e.

Essential Commentary on Mind training (*Sems sbyong don khrid*). In *sNying thig ya bzhi*. Reprint of the 'dzom 'brug pa chos sgar edition. Darjeeling: Talung Tsetrul Pema Wangyal, 1976.

Flower Ornament Sutra (*'Phags pa sdong po bkod pa'i mdo; Arya gandhavyuha sutra*). Section 45 of the *Buddha Avatamsaka Sutra*, pp. 117.1.5–315.1.1. See entry for *Buddha Avatamsaka Sutra.*

Great Chariot. (*rDzogs pa chen po sems nyid ngal gso' 'grel pa shing rta chen po*). Klong chen rab 'byams. This is Longchenpa's own commentary on *Resting in the Nature of Mind* (*rDzogs pa chen po sems nyid ngal gso*). In *rDzogs pa chen po ngal so skor gsum dang rang grol skor gsum dang bcas pod gsum*, vols. 1–2.

Guru's Quintessence (*Bla ma yang thig*). YS: vols. 1–2.

Heap of Jewels Sutra (*dKon mchog brtsegs pa chen po'i chos kyi rnam grangs le'u stong phrag brgya pa; Arya maharatnakuta dharmaparyaya shatasahasrika grantha*). PK: 0760, dkon brtsegs, tshi.

Jewel Rosary of Advice (*Zhal gdams nor bu'i phreng ba*). Source unknown.

Kshitigarbha Sutra (*'Dus pa chen po las sa'i snying po'i 'khor lo bcu pa zhes bya ba theg pa chen po'i mdo; Dashachakra kshitigarbhanama mahayana sutra*). DK: 0239, mdo sde, zha.

Lamp for the Path to Enlightenment (*Byang chub lam gyi sgron ma*; *Bodhipa-thapradipa*). By Atisha [A ti sha]. DT: 3947, dbu ma, khi.

Lamp That Clarifies Wisdom (*Ye shes gsal sgron*). In *sNying thig ya bzhi*. Reprint of the 'dzom 'brug pa chos sgar edition. Darjeeling: Talung Tse-trul Pema Wangyal, 1976.

Letter to a Friend (*bShes pa'i spring yig*; *Suhrllekha*). By Nagarjuna [Klu sgrub]. DT: 4496, jo bo'i chos chung, gi.

Letter to a Student (*sLob ma la springs pa*; *Shishyalekha*). By Chandragomin [Go mi dge bsnyen]. DT: 4183, spring yig, nge.

Luminous Tantra of Self-Arising Awareness (*'Od gsal gyi rgyud rig pa rang shar*). See *Tantra of Self-Arising Awareness*.

Meeting of Father and Son Sutra (*'Phags pa yab dang sras mjal ba zhes bya ba theg pa chen po'i mdo*; *Arya pita putra samagama nama mahayana sutra*). From the *Ratna-kuta Sutra*, PK: 760, vol. 23, dKon brtsegs 4, zhi.

Mother Tantra of the Clear Expanse (*Ma rgyud klong gsal*). See *Tantra of the Clear Expanse*.

Ornament of the Sutras (*Theg pa chen po mdo sde'i rgyan gyi tshig le'ur byas pa*; *Mahayanasutralamkarakarika*). DK: 4020, sems tsam, phi.

Precious Wish-Fulfilling Treasury (*Theg pa chen po'i man ngag gi bstan bcos yid bzhin rin po che'i mdzod*). By Klong chen rab 'byams, vol. 7 of *mDzod bdun*. Gangtok: Sherab Gyaltsen and Khyentse Labrang (based on the Oddiyana Institute edition of Tarthang Rinpoche), 1983.

Samantabhadra Tantra (*Kun tu bzang po'i rgyud*). There are many texts that this could refer to. The most likely choice, however, is this title from the *Collected Tantras of the Nyingma School*: (*lTa ba thams cad kyi rgyal po kun tu bzang po che ba la rang gnas pa'i rgyud*). NG: Tb. 93, vol. 4 (nga), text 9.

Sorrow-Dispelling Sutra (*Mya ngan bsal ba'i mdo*). Source unknown.

Sphere of Liberation (*Grol ba'i thig le zhes bya ba*; *Muktitilaka nama*). By Bud-dhajnanapada [Ye shes zhabs]. DK: 1859, di.

Sutra in Three Parts (*'Phags pa phung po gsum pa zhes bya ba theg pa chen po'i mdo*; *Arya triskandhaka nama mahayana sutra*). DK: 0284, mdo sde, ya.

Sutra of Advice to King Prasenajid (*gSal rgyal gyi tshigs su bcad pa*; *Prasena-jidgatha*). DK: 0322, mdo sde, sa.

Sutra of Advice to the King (*rGyal po la gdams pa zhes bya ba theg pa chen po'i mdo*; *Rajadesha nama mahayana sutra*). DK: 0214, mdo sde, tsha.

Sutra of One Hundred Actions (*Las brgya tham pa; Karmashataka*). DK: 0304, mdo sde, ha.

Sutra of the Vast Display (*'Phags pa rgya cher rol pa zhes bya ba theg pa chen po'i mdo*; *Arya lalita vistara nama mahayana sutra*). DK: 0095, mdo sde, kha.

Sutra Requested by Sagaramati (*'Phags pa blo gros rgya mtshos zhus ba zhes bya ba theg pa chen po'i mdo*; *Arya sagaramatipariprccha nama mahayana sutra*). DK: 0152, mdo sde, pha.

Sutra That Condenses the Precious Qualities of Realized Beings (*'Phags pa chos yang dag par sdud pa zhes bya ba theg pa chen po'i mdo*; *Arya dharmasamgiti nama mahayana sutra*). DK: 0238, mdo sde, zha.

Tantra of Self-Arising Awareness (*Rig pa rang shar chen po'i rgyud*). NG: 286, vol. 11 (da), Atiyoga.

Tantra of the Clear Expanse (*rGyud kyi rtse rgyal nyi zla 'od 'bar mkha' klong rnam dag rgya mtsho klong gsal rgyud*). NG: 270, vol. 10 (tha), Atiyoga.

Treasury of Higher Dharma (*Chos mngon pa'i mdzod kyi tshig le'ur byas pa*; *Abhidharma kosha karika*). By Vasubandhu [Dbyig gnyen]. DT: 4089, mngon pa, ku.

Treatise on the Levels (*Byang chub sems dpa'i sa*; *Bodhisattvabhumi*). By Asanga [Thogs med]. DT: 4037, sems tsam, wi.

Selected Bibliography

The following is a list of works that were either consulted when I was preparing the translations or cited in the notes or glossary. Please see the works cited list for the works cited by the authors of the texts translated in this volume.

WORKS IN THE ENGLISH LANGUAGE

Dahl, Cortland, ed. *Entrance to the Great Perfection*. Ithaca, N.Y.: Snow Lion Publications, 2009.

Dudjom Rinpoche. *The Nyingma School of Tibetan Buddhism*. Boston: Wisdom Publications, 1991.

Gampopa. *The Jewel Ornament of Liberation: The Wish-Fulfilling Gem of the Noble Teachings*. Ithaca, N.Y.: Snow Lion Publications, 1998.

Jamgön Kongtrul. *The Treasury of Knowledge: Book Six, Part Four: Systems of Buddhist Tantra*. Translated by the Kalu Rinpoché Translation Group (Elio Guarisco and Ingrid McLeod). Ithaca, N.Y.: Snow Lion Publications, 2005.

Jigme Lingpa, Patrul Rinpoche, and Getse Mahāpaṇḍita. *Deity, Mantra, and Wisdom: Development Stage Meditation in Tibetan Buddhist Tantra*. Ithaca, N.Y.: Snow Lion Publications, 2007.

Khenpo Ngawang Pelzang. *Guide to the Words of My Perfect Teacher*. Boston: Shambhala Publications, 2004.

Longchen Rabjam. *The Excellent Path to Enlightenment*. Translated by Khenpo Gawang Rinpoche and Gerry Wiener. Jeweled Lotus Publishing, 2014.

———. *The Practice of Dzogchen*. Introduced, translated, and annotated by Tulku Thondup. Ithaca, N.Y.: Snow Lion Publications, 2002.

Nyoshul Khenpo Jamyang Dorje. *A Marvelous Garland of Rare Gems*. Junction City, Calif.: Padma Publishing, 2005.

Padmasambhava and Jamgön Kongtrül. *Light of Wisdom*. Vol. 2. Hong Kong: Rangjung Yeshe Publications, 1998.

Patrul Rinpoche. *Words of My Perfect Teacher*. New Haven, Conn.: Yale University Press, 2010.

Third Dzogchen Rinpoche. *Great Perfection: Outer and Inner Preliminaries*. Ithaca, N.Y.: Snow Lion Publications, 2007.

———. *Great Perfection*. Vol. 2, *Separation and Breakthrough*. Ithaca, N.Y.: Snow Lion Publications, 2008.

Thupten Jinpa, ed. *Mind training: The Great Collection*. Boston: Wisdom Publications, 2006.

Tsele Natsok Rangdröl. "The Ripening Empowerments." In *Dzogchen Essentials*, compiled and edited by Marcia Binder Schmidt and translated by Erik Pema Kunsang, 27–37. Hong Kong: Rangjung Yeshe Publications, 2004.

Tsong-kha-pa. *The Great Treatise on the Stages of the Path to Enlightenment*. 3 vols. Ithaca, N.Y.: Snow Lion Publications, 2000–2004.

Tulku Thondup. *Masters of Meditation and Miracles*. Boston: Shambhala Publications, 1996.

WORKS IN THE TIBETAN LANGUAGE

Jamgön Kongtrul ('Jam mgon kong sprul). *Pristine Advice* (*rDzogs pa chen po gsang ba snying thig ma bu'i bka' srol chu bo gnyis 'dus kyi khrid yig dri med zhal lung*). In *rNying ma bka' ma rgyas pa*, vol. Wa. Kalimpong, India: Dupjung Lama, 1982.

———. *Treasury of Knowledge* (*Shes bya kun khyab*). Beijing: Mi rigs dpe skrun khang, 1982.

Jamyang Khyentse Wangpo ('Jam dbyangs mkhyen brtse dbang po). *The Chetsun Nyingtik Cycle* (*lCe btsun snying thig gi chos skor*). Darjeeling: Taklung Tsetrul Pema Wangyal, 1985.

Jigme Lingpa ('Jigs med gling pa). *Chariot of Omniscience* (*Yon tan rin po che'i mdzod las 'bras bu'i theg pa rgya cher 'grel rnam mkhyen shing rta*). Kathmandu: Shechen Monastery, n.d.

———. *Light Rays of Wisdom and Love* (*Bla ma dgongs pa 'dus pa'i cho ga'i rnam bzhag dang 'brel ba'i bskyed rdzogs zung 'jug gi sgron ma mkhyen brtse'i me long 'od zer brgya pa*). Paro, Bhutan: Lama Ngodrup and Sherab Demy, 1985.

———. *Ornament of All Jambudvipa* (*De bzhin gshegs pas legs par gsungs pa'i gsung rab rgya mtsho'i snying por gyur pa rig pa 'dzin pa'i sde snod dam/ snga 'gyur rgyud 'bum rin po che'i rtogs pa brjod pa 'dzam gling tha gru khyab pa'i rgyan*). In *'Jigs med gling pa'i gsung 'bum*, vol. 13 (pa). Paro, Bhutan: Lama Ngodrup and Sherab Demy, 1985.

———. *Staircase to Akanishta* (*bsKyed rim lha'i khrid kyi rnam par bzhag pa 'og min bgrod pa'i them skas*). Gangtok, Sikkim: Dodrupchen Monastery, n.d.

———. *Steps to Liberation* (*Thun mong gi sngon 'gro sems sbyong rnam pa bdun gyi don khrid thar ba'i them skas*). Paro, Bhutan: Lama Ngodrup and Sherab Demy, 1985.

———. *Steps to Liberation* (*Thun mong gi sngon 'gro sems sbyong rnam pa bdun gyi don khrid thar ba'i them skas*). Gantok, Sikkim: Pema Thinley, 1985.

———. *Yeshe Lama* (*rDzogs pa chen po klong chen snying tig gi gdod ma'i mgon po'i lam gyi rim pa'i khrid yig ye shes bla ma*). In *rDzogs chen skor gsum*. Kathmandu: bLa ma phrin las dgon, 1999.

Ju Mipam Gyatso ('Ju mi pham rgya mtsho). *Essence of Luminosity* (*Gsang 'grel phyogs bcu'i mun sel gyi spyi don 'od gsal snying po*). Chengdu, China: Si khron mi rigs dpe skrun khang, 2000.

———. *Essence of Siddhi* (*dPal sgrub pa chen po bka' brgyad kyi spyi don rnam par bshad pa dngos grub snying po*). Chengdu, China: Si khron mi rigs dpe skrun khang, 2000.

———. *Gateway to Knowledge* (*mKhas pa'i tshul la 'jug pa'i sgo*). Qinghai, China: mTsho sngon mi rigs dpe skrun khang, 2003.

———. *Rosary of Light Rays* (*dBus dang mtha' rnam par 'byed pa'i bstan bcos kyi 'grel pa 'od zer phreng ba*). In *'Jam mgon 'ju mi pham rgya mtsho'i gsung 'bum rgyas pa sde dge dgon chen par ma*, vol. 4. Paro, Bhutan: Lama Ngodrup and Sherab Demy, 1984.

Longchen Rabjam (Klong chen rab 'byams). *Clouds on the Ocean of the Profound Meaning* (*Zab don rgya mtsho' sprin*). In *sNying thig ya bzhi*, vol. 1. Unpublished electronic version. Kathmandu: Nitartha Input Center, n.d.

———. *Dispelling Darkness of the Ten Directions* (*dPal gsang ba'i snying po de kho na nyid nges pa'i rgyud kyi 'grel pa phyogs bcu'i mun pa thams cad rnam par sel ba*). Electronic publication. Kathmandu: Shechen Publications, 1998.

———. *Great Chariot* (*rDzogs pa chen po sems nyid ngal gso'i 'grel pa shing rta chen po*). Scanned edition based on the prints from A'dzom 'brug pa chos sgar. New York: Tibetan Buddhist Resource Center, 1999.

———. *Illuminating Sun* (*bsTan pa bu gcig gi rgyud gser gyi snying po nyi ma rab tu snang byed*). In *sNying thig ya bzhi*. Reprint of the A'dzom 'brug pa chos sgar edition. Darjeeling: Taklung Tsetrul Pema Wangyal, 1976.

———. *Precious Treasury of the Supreme Vehicle* (*Theg pa'i mchog rin po che'i mdzod*). Gangtok, Sikkim: Sherab Gyaltsen and Khyentse Labrang, 1983.

————. *Precious Wish-Fulfilling Treasury* (*Theg pa chen po'i man ngag gi bstan bcos yid bzhin rin po che'i mdzod*). Gangtok, Sikkim: Sherab Gyaltsen and Khyentse Labrang, 1983.

————. *Resting in the Nature of Mind* (*rDzogs pa chen po sems nyid ngal gso*). In *rDzogs pa chen po ngal so skor gsum dang rang grol skor gsum dang bcas pod gsum.* Scanned edition of the prints from A'dzom 'brug pa chos sgar. New York: Tibetan Buddhist Resource Center, 1999.

————. *Secret Commentary on the "Tantra of the Sole Offspring"* (*bTags pas grol bar stan pa bu gcig gi gsang 'grel slob dpon dga' rab rdo rjes mdzad pa*). In *sNying thig ya bzhi.* Reprint of the A'dzom 'brug pa chos sgar edition. Darjeeling: Talung Tsetrul Pema Wangyal, 1976.

————. *Seven Mind trainings: Essential Instructions on the Preliminary Practices* (*sNgon 'gro sems byong bdun gyi don khrid*). In *sNying thig ya bzhi.* Reprint of the A'dzom 'brug pa chos sgar edition. Darjeeling: Talung Tsetrul Pema Wangyal, 1976.

————. *Treasury of Transmissions* (*Chos dbyings rin po che'i mdzod kyi 'grel pa lung gi gter mdzod*). Gangtok, Sikkim: Sherab Gyaltsen and Khyentse Labrang, 1983.

Ngedon Tenzin Zangpo (Nges don bstan 'dzin bzang po). *Excellent Chariot* (*rDzogs pa chen po mkha' 'gro snying thig gi khrid yig thar lam bgrod byed shing rta bzang po*). Chengdu, China: Si khron mi rigs dpe skrun khang, 1997.

Patrul Orgyen Chokyi Wangpo (dPal sprul O rgyan chos kyi dbang po). *Words of My Perfect Teacher* (*rDzogs pa chen po klong chen snying thig gi sngon 'gro'i khrid yig kun bzang bla ma'i zhal lung*). dPal sprul O rgyan chos kyi dbang po'i gsung 'bum, vol. 7. Chengdu, China: Si khron mi rigs dpe skrun khang, 2003.

Trang Chi Sun (Krang dbyi sun), ed. *Great Tibetan-Chinese Dictionary* (*Bod rgya tshig mdzod chen mo*). Chengdu, China: Si khron mi rigs dpe skrun khang, 1988.

Recommended Reading

Contemporary Presentations

Chagdud Tulku. *Gates to Buddhist Practice: Essential Teachings of a Tibetan Master*. Junction City, Calif.: Padma Publishing, 2001.

Chögyam Trungpa. *Cutting Through Spiritual Materialism*. Boston: Shambhala Publications, 2002.

Dzongsar Jamyang Khyentse. *What Makes You Not a Buddhist*. Boston: Shambhala Publications, 2008.

Khandro Rinpoche. *This Precious Life: Tibetan Buddhist Teachings on the Path to Enlightenment*. Boston: Shambhala Publications, 2005.

Ray, Reginald. *Indestructible Truth: The Living Spirituality of Tibetan Buddhism*. Boston: Shambhala Publications, 2000.

———. *Secret of the Vajra World: The Tantric Buddhism of Tibet*. Boston: Shambhala Publications, 2001.

Sogyal Rinpoche. *The Tibetan Book of Living and Dying*. New York: HarperCollins, 1994.

Thinley Norbu. *The Small Golden Key*. Boston: Shambhala Publications, 1993.

Thubten Yeshe. *Introduction to Tantra: The Transformation of Desire*. Boston: Wisdom Publications, 2001.

Yongey Mingyur Rinpoche. *The Joy of Living: Unlocking the Secret and Science of Happiness*. New York: Three Rivers Press, 2008.

———. *Turning Confusion into Clarity: A Guide to the Foundation Practices of Tibetan Buddhism*. Boston: Snow Lion, 2014.

Traditional Instructions

Dilgo Khyentse Rinpoche. *The Heart of Compassion: The Thirty-Seven Verses on the Practice of a Bodhisattva*. Boston: Shambhala Publications, 2007.

———. *The Heart Treasure of the Enlightened Ones: The Practice of View, Meditation, and Action*. Boston: Shambhala Publications, 1993.

Jamgön Mipham. *White Lotus: An Explanation of the Seven-Line Prayer to Guru Padmasambhava*. Boston: Shambhala Publications, 2007.

Kangyur Rinpoche. *Treasury of Precious Qualities*. Boston: Shambhala Publications, 2001.

Kunzang Pelden. *The Nectar of Manjushri's Speech: A Detailed Commentary on Shantideva's "Way of the Bodhisattva."* Boston: Shambhala Publications, 2007.

Padmasambhava. *Advice from the Lotus-Born: A Collection of Padmasambhava's Advice to the Dakini Yeshe Tsogyal and Other Close Disciples*. Hong Kong: Rangjung Yeshe Publications, 1994.

———. *Dakini Teachings*. Hong Kong: Rangjung Yeshe Publications, 1999.

Shabkar. *Food of Bodhisattvas: Buddhist Teachings on Abstaining from Meat*. Boston: Shambhala Publications, 2004.

Shantideva. *The Way of the Bodhisattva*. Boston: Shambhala Publications, 2008.

Thrangu Rinpoche. *The Practice of Tranquillity and Insight: A Guide to Tibetan Buddhist Meditation*. Boston: Shambhala Publications, 1994.

HISTORY AND BIOGRAPHY

Allione, Tsultrim. *Women of Wisdom*. Ithaca, N.Y.: Snow Lion Publications, 2000.

Chagdud Tulku. *Lord of the Dance: Autobiography of a Tibetan Lama*. Junction City, Calif.: Padma Publishing, 1992.

Chatral Rinpoche. *Compassionate Action*. Ithaca, N.Y.: Snow Lion Publications, 2007.

Dilgo Khyentse. *Brilliant Moon: The Autobiography of Dilgo Khyentse*. Boston: Shambhala Publications, 2008.

Dudjom Rinpoche. *The Nyingma School of Tibetan Buddhism: Its Fundamentals and History*. Boston: Wisdom Publications, 1991.

Gyalwa Changchub. *Lady of the Lotus-Born: The Life and Enlightenment of Yeshe Tsogyal*. Boston: Shambhala Publications, 2002.

Kunsang, Erik Pema. *Wellsprings of the Great Perfection: The Lives and Insights of the Early Masters*. Hong Kong: Rangjung Yeshe Publications, 2006.

Ngawang Zangpo. *Guru Rinpoche: His Life and Times*. Ithaca, N.Y.: Snow Lion Publications, 2002.

Nyoshul Khenpo Jamyang Dorjé. *A Marvelous Garland of Rare Gems: Biographies of Masters of Awareness in the Dzogchen Lineage*. Junction City, Calif.: Padma Publishing, 2005.

Sangye Khandro. *The Lives and Liberation of Princess Mandarava: The Indian Consort of Padmasambhava.* Boston: Wisdom Publications, 1998.
Shabkar Tsogdruk Rangdrol. *The Life of Shabkar: The Autobiography of a Tibetan Yogin.* Ithaca, N.Y.: Snow Lion Publications, 2001.
Thich Nhat Hanh. *Old Path White Clouds: Walking in the Footsteps of the Buddha.* Berkeley: Parallax Press, 1991.
Tulku Thondup. *Hidden Teachings of Tibet: An Explanation of the Terma Tradition of Tibetan Buddhism.* Boston: Wisdom Publications, 1997.
———. *Masters of Meditation and Miracles.* Boston: Shambhala Publications, 1999.
Tulku Urgyen Rinpoche. *Blazing Splendor: The Memoirs of Tulku Urgyen Rinpoche.* Hong Kong: Rangjung Yeshe Publications, 2005.
Yeshe Tsogyal. *The Lotus-Born: The Life Story of Padmasambhava.* Boston: Shambhala Publications, 1992.
Yudra Nyingpo. *The Great Image: The Life Story of Vairochana the Translator.* Boston: Shambhala Publications, 2004.

PRELIMINARY PRACTICES

Chagdud Tulku. *Ngöndro Commentary: Instructions for the Concise Preliminary Practices of the New Treasure of Dudjom.* Junction City, Calif.: Padma Publishing, 1995.
Dahl, Cortland, ed. *Entrance to the Great Perfection: A Guide to the Dzogchen Preliminary Practices.* Ithaca, N.Y.: Snow Lion Publications, 2010.
Dilgo Khyentse. *Guru Yoga: According to the Preliminary Practice of Longchen Nyingtik.* Ithaca, N.Y.: Snow Lion Publications, 1999.
———. *The Excellent Path to Enlightenment: Oral Teachings on the Root Text of Jamyang Khyentse Wangpo.* Ithaca, N.Y.: Snow Lion Publications, 1996.
———. *The Wish-Fulfilling Jewel: The Practice of Guru Yoga according to the Longchen Nyingthig Tradition.* Boston: Shambhala Publications, 1999.
Dzongsar Jamyang Khyentse. *Not for Happiness: A Guide to the So-Salled Preliminary Practices.* Boston: Shambhala Publications, 2012.
Khenpo Ngawang Pelzang. *A Guide to "The Words of My Perfect Teacher."* Boston: Shambhala Publications, 2004.
Klein, Anne. *Heart Essence of the Vast Expanse: A Story of Transmission.* Ithaca, N.Y.: Snow Lion Publications, 2010.
Padmasambhava and Jamgön Kongtrül. *The Light of Wisdom.* Vol. 1. Kathmandu: Rangjung Yeshe Publications, 1986.

Patrul Rinpoche. *The Words of My Perfect Teacher*. Boston: Shambhala Publications, 1998.

Thinley Norbu. *A Cascading Waterfall of Nectar*. Boston: Shambhala Publications, 2006.

Third Dzogchen Rinpoche. *Great Perfection: Outer and Inner Preliminaries*. Ithaca, N.Y.: Snow Lion Publications, 2007.

Yongey Mingyur Rinpoche. *Turning Confusion into Clarity: A Guide to the Foundation Practices of Tibetan Buddhism*. Boston: Snow Lion, 2014.

DEVELOPMENT STAGE MEDITATION

Gyatrul Rinpoche. *The Generation Stage in Buddhist Tantra*. Ithaca, N.Y.: Snow Lion Publications, 2005.

Jamgön Kongtrül. *Creation and Completion: Essential Points of Tantric Meditation*. Boston: Wisdom Publications, 2002.

Jigme Lingpa, Patrul Rinpoche, and Getse Mahāpaṇḍita. *Deity, Mantra, and Wisdom: Development Stage Meditation in Tibetan Buddhist Tantra*. Ithaca, N.Y.: Snow Lion Publications, 2007.

Khenpo Namdrol Rinpoche. *The Practice of Vajrakilaya*. Ithaca, N.Y.: Snow Lion Publications, 1999.

Kunkyen Tenpe Nyima and Shechen Gyaltsap IV. *Vajra Wisdom: Deity Practice in Tibetan Buddhism*. Boston: Snow Lion Publications, 2013.

Padmasambhava and Jamgön Kongtrül. *The Light of Wisdom*. Vol. 1. Kathmandu: Rangjung Yeshe Publications, 1986.

GREAT PERFECTION

Chögyal Namkhai Norbu. *The Crystal and the Way of Light: Sutra, Tantra, and Dzogchen*. Ithaca, N.Y.: Snow Lion Publications, 1999.

Chökyi Nyima Rinpoche. *Present Fresh Wakefulness: A Meditation Manual on Nonconceptual Wisdom*. Hong Kong: Rangjung Yeshe Publications, 2002.

The Dalai Lama. *Mind in Comfort and Ease: The Vision of Enlightenment in the Great Perfection*. Boston: Wisdom Publications, 2007.

Drubwang Tsoknyi Rinpoche. *Carefree Dignity: Discourses on Training in the Nature of Mind*. Hong Kong: Rangjung Yeshe Publications, 1998.

———. *Fearless Simplicity: The Dzogchen Way of Living Freely in a Complex World*. Hong Kong: Rangjung Yeshe Publications, 2003.

Dudjom Lingpa. *Buddhahood without Meditation: A Visionary Account Known as "Refining Apparent Phenomena."* Rev. ed. Junction City, Calif.: Padma Publishing, 2002.

RECOMMENDED READING — 163

———. *The Vajra Essence.* Austin: Palri Parkhang, 2004.

Dzogchen Ponlop Rinpoche. *Wild Awakening: The Heart of Mahamudra and Dzogchen.* Boston: Shambhala Publications, 2003.

Karma Chagmé. *Naked Awareness: Practical Instructions on the Union of Mahāmudrā and Dzogchen.* Ithaca, N.Y.: Snow Lion Publications, 2000.

———. *A Spacious Path to Freedom: Practical Instructions on the Union of Mahāmudrā and Atiyoga.* Ithaca, N.Y.: Snow Lion Publications, 1997.

Khamtrul Rinpoche. *Dzogchen Meditation.* Dharamsala, India: Library of Tibetan Works and Archives, 2004.

Longchen Rabjam. *The Practice of Dzogchen.* Introduced, translated, and annotated by Tulku Thondup. Ithaca, N.Y.: Snow Lion Publications, 2002.

———. *The Precious Treasury of the Basic Space of Phenomena.* Junction City, Calif.: Padma Publishing, 2001.

———. *The Precious Treasury of the Way of Abiding.* Junction City, Calif.: Padma Publishing, 1998.

———. *A Treasure Trove of Scriptural Transmission.* Junction City, Calif.: Padma Publishing, 2001.

Namkhai Norbu. *The Cycle of Day and Night: Where One Proceeds along the Path of the Primordial Yoga: An Essential Tibetan Text on the Practice of Dzogchen.* Barrytown, N.Y.: Station Hill Press, 2000.

Padmasambhava and Jamgön Kongtrül. *The Light of Wisdom.* Vol. 4. Kathmandu: Rangjung Yeshe Publications, 1986.

Padmasambhava et al. *Crystal Cave.* Kathmandu: Rangjung Yeshe Publications, 1990.

Shabkar Tsokdruk Rangdrol et al. *The Flight of the Garuda.* Kathmandu: Rangjung Yeshe Publications, 1993.

Third Dzogchen Rinpoche. *Great Perfection.* Vol. 2, *Separation and Breakthrough.* Ithaca, N.Y.: Snow Lion Publications, 2008.

Tsele Natsok Rangdrol. *Circle of the Sun.* Kathmandu: Rangjung Yeshe Publications, 1990.

Tulku Urgyen Rinpoche. *Quintessential Dzogchen: Confusion Dawns as Wisdom.* Hong Kong: Rangjung Yeshe Publications, 2006.

———. *Rainbow Painting: A Collection of Miscellaneous Aspects of Development and Completion.* Hong Kong: Rangjung Yeshe Publications, 1995.

van Schaik, Sam. *Approaching the Great Perfection: Simultaneous and Gradual Methods of Dzogchen Practice in the Longchen Nyingtig.* Boston: Wisdom Publications, 2003.

Vidyādhara Jigmed Lingpa. *Yeshe Lama.* Ithaca, N.Y.: Snow Lion Publications, 2009.

PHILOSOPHY

Arya Maitreya. *Buddha Nature: "The Mahayana Uttaratantra Shastra" with Commentary.* Ithaca, N.Y.: Snow Lion Publications, 2000. See also under Maitreya.

Jamgön Mipham. *The Adornment of the Middle Way: Shantarakshita's "Madhyamakalankara" with Commentary by Jamgön Mipham.* Boston: Shambhala Publications, 2005.

————. *Introduction to the Middle Way: Chandrakirti's "Madhyamakavatara" with Commentary by Jamgön Mipham.* Boston: Shambhala Publications, 2005.

————. *Luminous Essence: A Guide to the Guhyagarbha Tantra.* Ithaca, N.Y.: Snow Lion Publications, 2009.

————. *Speech of Delight: Mipham's Commentary on Shantarakshita's "Ornament of the Middle Way."* Ithaca, N.Y.: Snow Lion Publications, 2004.

Köppl, Heidi. *Establishing Appearances as Divine: Rongzom Chokyi Zangpo on Reasoning, Madhyamaka, and Purity.* Ithaca, N.Y.: Snow Lion Publications, 2008.

Mabja Jangchub Tsöndrü. *Ornament of Reason: The Great Commentary to Nagarjuna's "Root of The Middle Way."* Ithaca, N.Y.: Snow Lion Publications, 2011.

Maitreya. *Distinguishing Phenomena from Their Intrinsic Nature: Maitreya's "Dharmadharmatāvibhaṅga" with Commentaries by Khenpo Shenga and Ju Mipham.* Boston: Snow Lion, 2013. See also under Arya Maitreya.

————. *Middle Beyond Extremes: Maitreya's "Madhyāntavibhāga" with Commentaries by Khenpo Shenga and Ju Mipham.* Ithaca, N.Y.: Snow Lion Publications, 2007.

————. *Ornament of the Great Vehicle Sutras: Maitreya's "Mahāyānasūtrālaṃkāra" with Commentaries by Khenpo Shenga and Ju Mipham.* Boston: Snow Lion, 2014.

Pettit, John. *Mipham's "Beacon of Certainty": Illuminating the View of Dzogchen.* Boston: Wisdom Publications, 1999.

Index

Saving the Lives of Animals

All royalties from the sale of this book will be used to save the lives of animals that would otherwise be killed. If you would like to make a tax-deductible donation for this purpose, please e-mail savinglives@tergar.org.